40 GREAT TENNIS SESSIONS

Peter Farrell

Published by Tennis Ireland Coaches Association

Copyright © Peter Farrell 2010

First published in Ireland in 2010 by
TICA - Tennis Ireland Coaches Association (www.tica.ie)

A CIP catalogue record for this book is available from the British Library

ISBN 978-0-9567160-0-2

Printed and bound in Ireland by Gemini International Limited

CONTENTS

INTRODUCTION

'Drills are the basic elements that define the structure of all tennis practices.'
***Tennis Psychology*, International Tennis Federation (2006)**

Why do people play tennis? Research tells us that the overriding motive is 'to have fun'. Fun stems from playing the game and experiencing the excitement of rallying, and from the challenge of competing at the appropriate level. This game-based approach to tennis is personified in the International Tennis Federation's Play and Stay programme, which centres around the slogan 'Serve, rally and score', and the recommendation that starter players play the game from the first lesson.

I have always believed that playing the game is the best way to keep people involved in tennis, while providing opportunities to point out what they need to do in order to further develop their ability. So if this is the case, is there a need for a book like this?

Effective drills serve many purposes in a tennis session. They provide variety and deliver competitive opportunities in a microcosm. They allow players to improve weaknesses and further develop strengths, removed from the pressures of matchplay. Most importantly, they allow players to make repeated attempts at essential strokes, patterns and tactics. From repeated practice comes competence, and from competence flows the confidence to integrate newly acquired skills back into matchplay.

Each chapter of *40 Great Tennis Sessions* contains a series of exercises or drills relating to a particular shot or tactic. As a general rule each exercise is a progression from the previous one. This design leads a player forward in a series of small steps, ensuring fast understanding and improvement. Taken as a whole, the exercises in each chapter provide a complete on-court practice session for an important tennis skill. All of the exercises are proven to be effective; I have fine-tuned them on court in the course of my thirty years teaching the game. I hope that from the exercises contained in the pages that follow you will be able to generate many more, using your experience and knowledge to add progressions and developments to the situations presented here.

What is in my opinion one of the most positive developments ever in tennis occurred recently with the introduction by the International Tennis Federation of the red, orange and green balls and courts. Lighter balls and smaller courts make the game much easier to introduce to children and starter adults. Almost all the exercises in this book can be used on the red, orange or green court.

Use the corresponding ball to allow even inexperienced players to explore facets of the game that would previously have been closed to them until much later in their development. You can access full details of the three stages at www.tennisplayandstay.com.

At the start of each chapter I have used the International Tennis Number (ITN) to suggest the level of player at which the exercises are aimed. The ITN is an initiative that was introduced in 2004 by the International Tennis Federation. A player is given a rating from 1 to 10. Someone with a rating of 10, 9 or 8 is considered a Recreational Level player; a rating of 7, 6 or 5 denotes an Intermediate Level player; while 4, 3 or 2 indicates an Advanced Level player. An ITN rating of 1 suggests a world-class player, capable of competing on the men's or women's pro circuit.

However, you may be able to make the exercises in this book relevant to a lower or higher standard of player than I suggest by adapting the rules, adding in or taking out shots, or changing target areas. So the ITN rating at the start of each chapter should be regarded as a guide and not set in stone. Many nations have adopted the ITN as their official rating system and at time of writing there are on-court ITN Assessors in one hundred and nine countries. You can read more about the programme at www.itftennis.com/itn.

When playing tennis, nothing is more important than safety. Before carrying out any of the exercises in this book, players should perform a thorough warm-up. A medical check up is recommended before undertaking any form of strenuous exercise.

Please note that, for the purpose of clarity, I have used the words 'he', 'him' and 'his' throughout this book. However, every reference to the masculine includes the feminine gender.

I want to thank the following people for their help in making this book come together. Aoife Kennedy for typesetting and design, and Ruth Kennedy for proofreading. Also Liam Cassidy and Paul Murphy of TICA for supporting the project from the start.

I would like to dedicate this book to Colette, Daniel and Sean.

Peter Farrell

PART ONE:
SERVE AND RETURN

SERVING FOR BEGINNERS

PLAYING STANDARD: ITN 10-8

The serve is a shot that often causes problems for beginner players: some find it difficult to coordinate the movement of both arms at the same time; there is the challenge of tossing the ball up accurately when you have to use your 'wrong' hand. However, whether you are learning or teaching this shot, it is always a good idea to focus on the positives. The serve is unique in tennis in several ways:
- You get two chances.
- You have total control of the ball; your opponent has no real influence over the shot.
- Time is on your side: there is no rush to get to the ball before it bounces twice.
- It is the one shot you can practice effectively while alone on court.

THROW TO SERVE

Start each point by throwing the ball overarm into the service box. Then the rally continues with racquets as normal.

 The overarm throwing action is very similar to the overarm service action.

FOUR TOSS TEST

The player tosses the ball up as if to serve, but lets it bounce instead. He then uses the ball to mark the spot on the court where the ball bounced. Repeat this process another three times. Can the player 'cover' the four balls with the face of his racquet? This is a good indication of the player's level of accuracy with the toss.

'Release' rather than 'throw'.

The elbow and wrist of the tossing arm should be kept straight.

SOLO SERVE

The player plays a set against himself, using only serves. If the first or second serve is in, the player wins the point. If it is a double fault, the player loses the point.

This exercise underlines the principle that the serve is under the absolute control of the server; there is no influence or input from the receiver.

SERVICE GOLF

This exercise follows the same principles as a game of golf: hit the ball into all the 'holes' using as few shots as possible. Use three courts and all twelve service boxes.

Player serves to box number one. If he gets it in, his score is one and he moves on to service box number two. However, if the serve is not in, he stays at box number one and serves until he does get it in. The winner is the player using the fewest shots to get a serve into all twelve service boxes. Alternatively, how far along the 'course' can the player get using a total of twelve serves?

As in golf, there is no time restriction in this game.

Players should be encouraged to use their normal service ritual before each shot and to take as many attempts at the toss as they need.

DEEP SERVE

Players serve to the target areas as in the diagram. Who can score the most points from ten balls?

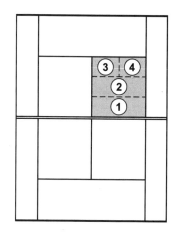

 Only one person in ten is left-handed; so only one tennis player in ten is left-handed.

The ability to serve deep to the right-hander's backhand will always be a staple shot for every player.

STEP BY STEP

A player hits one serve into the service box. If he does not get it in, he is 'stuck' on one and tries again to get one serve in on his next turn. If the first attempt is in, on his next turn he must serve two in a row into the box. If both serves are in, he moves on to three in his next round. However, if either of the two serves are faults, he is stuck on two for the next round. The first player to get five serves in a row into the designated service box wins the game.

 As with all aspects of tennis, consistency is crucial.

WHERE'S THE CATCH?

Player A serves to Player B, who tries to catch the ball. If the serve is in and B cannot catch it after one bounce, A scores a point. See how many points A can score from ten serves; then the players switch roles.

This is a good introduction to the importance of power and accuracy.

Accuracy can be further emphasised by instructing the catcher to stay in a particular spot, for example inside the tramlines, until the server has made contact with the ball.

SERVING TO WIN

Most experts agree that the serve is the single-most important shot in tennis. A strong serve can set a player up for an easy winner on the second shot, or even win the point without the opponent hitting the ball. It is a shot that need not and should not be rushed. Each player should develop an individualised ritual of bouncing the ball a set number of times before serving. This gives the server time to decide what type of serve to hit, where to hit it to and whether to stay back or serve and volley.

READ THE RECEIVER

The receiver of the serve is told by the coach to play a certain way, for example:
• stand very far back to receive;
• return with slice to the server's backhand;
• go down the line on the forehand return.

The job of the server is to discover as quickly as possible what the receiver has been asked to do, and then tell the coach.

 Part of the server's task is to analyse the quality and type of returns, and then use this information to make his serve more effective.

TELL THE RECEIVER

The service box is marked off as shown in the diagram. Three different coloured cones are placed near the net, one in each of the three service box areas. Before the server hits his shot, he calls out to his opponent which of the three targets he intends to aim for (for example 'red'). If the serve does not land in the designated area, it is a fault. Play on if it does bounce in the correct area.

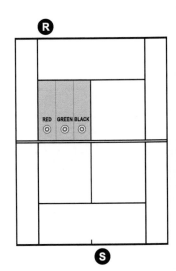

R

RED GREEN BLACK

S

Players often serve without making a conscious decision on a precise target zone. Using this exercise helps a coach discover which target areas a player is comfortable serving to.

HOLD

Play points where the server continues to serve until he loses the point. Keep the score numerically.

 The concept of 'holding serve' is vital in tennis. If your serve cannot be broken, you cannot lose the match.

IN DISGUISE

The coach stands near the server. *After* the server tosses the ball up, the coach tells him where to hit the serve to – forehand, backhand or 'body'.

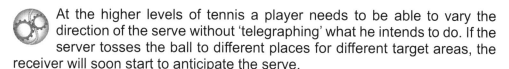 At the higher levels of tennis a player needs to be able to vary the direction of the serve without 'telegraphing' what he intends to do. If the server tosses the ball to different places for different target areas, the receiver will soon start to anticipate the serve.

PLAYING THE PERCENTAGES

Players should have an idea of their percentage of first serves in, so they know if they are serving with the optimum balance of power and control.

Two racquets, A and B, are placed behind the server, each with ten balls on it. The server takes a ball from racquet A for his first serve and from racquet B for his second serve. At the end of ten rallies, the number of balls left on racquet B (say six) is equal to the percentage of first serves in (60 per cent). Six out of the ten balls on racquet B were not used for second serves because six out of ten first serves were in.

At professional level, 60 to 70 per cent of first serves are into play. Any higher and the server is not 'going for it'.

This exercise can also be used to check how many points a player wins when he gets his first serve in versus how many he wins when he misses his first serve.

TWO FOR ONE

The server scores two points if he wins the rally having got his first serve in. He scores one point if he wins the rally following a second serve.

Alternatively, the receiver scores two points if he wins the rally off a second serve and one if he wins the rally off a first serve.

 This encourages the server to get a high percentage of first serves into play.

HORSE

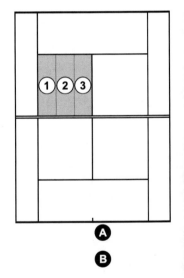

Two servers (A and B) take turns to serve from the same end of the court. Player A designates a target area (one, two or three). If A serves to the correct target area, B has to hit a serve to the same target area. If B's serve goes out of play, or to a different target area, he is on 'H'. In the next round, player B gets to decide on the target area. The first player to spell 'HORSE' loses the game.

 Players must develop the ability to serve to any part of the service box.

THE BIG SERVE

A player with a 'big serve' can win points outright with just one shot or often has an easy put-away on his second shot due to a weak return. It is a great shot to have in your armoury. In terms of the mental game, nothing boosts a player like hitting a series of unreturnable serves, and the effect on the receiving end can be devastating.

DEEP WINS

To win the point, the receiver only has to return the ball deep (bouncing past the service line). The server is forced to go for an ace or a winning serve.

 Unreturnable serves are often hit with lots of power, but good placement at a medium pace can also be effective.

FIFTY FROM TEN?

Server and receiver play ten points, with the same player serving all the time. The server scores:
- five points for an ace;
- three points for a winning serve (receiver makes contact with the ball, but does not return it into court);
- one point if he wins following a rally.

Server and receiver then switch roles, and the new server tries to beat his opponent's total score.

 After ten serves, a good server will have hit two or three that were unreturnable.

The coach can agree a target with the player, for example: 'Your goal is to score twenty points or more.'

SECOND FIRST SERVE

Play points where the server has three serves per rally – two first serves and a second serve.

 Servers are encouraged to go for it on the 'first first serve'.

SERVE FOR TEN

Server and receiver play ten points, with the same player serving all the time. The server starts with ten points.
- If he serves an ace, he adds two points to his score.
- If he hits a winning serve, he adds one point to his score.
- If the serve is returned, his score does not change.
- If he hits a fault, he subtracts one point from his score.

Server and receiver then switch roles and the new server tries to beat his opponent's total score.

 A coach can tell a player that he needs to improve his service speed and effectiveness, but it is better if the player discovers this himself. The best way to achieve this is by putting the player in situations where he can realistically assess the effectiveness or otherwise of his serve.

ON THE TABLE

A table is laid on its side as shown in the photograph. The server tries to hit the table and make the ball bounce back over the net to the server's side of the court.

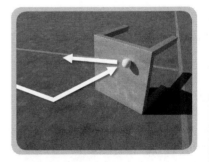

Vary the size and placement of the table.

THREE OR OUT

The player serving has to win the point before his fourth shot, with the serve counting as the first shot. If the server hasn't finished the rally before his fourth shot, the receiver wins the point.

If the serve is returned, the server should be looking for an opportunity to use his favourite put-away (for example crosscourt forehand) on his second shot. Ask the server to discover what type of serve is most likely to produce this result.

THE SECOND SERVE

Key facts on the second serve:
- If you miss it, you have given your opponent the point without him having to do anything.
- If you have a good second serve, you will have the confidence to really hit out on your first serve.
- If you do not have a good second serve, you will be tempted to play safe on the first serve.

KNEEL

Player kneels on one knee to hit the serve with topspin; then he stands up to continue the rally.

 Putting topspin on the serve greatly increases the chances of it going in. This exercise forces the player to 'hit up', which helps generate topspin.

SHORT AND WIDE (1)

Right-handed players take turns to serve to the deuce court. The serve that hits the side fence *nearest the net* wins. Stick the ball into the wire to mark the spot where it hit the fence.

 The server should sometimes move in for a volley after this type of serve. This can lead to an easy shot to the open court and will keep the receiver guessing on subsequent points.

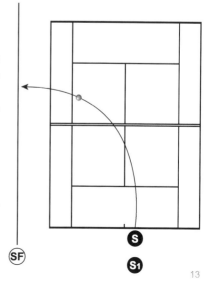

UP AND OVER

Players hit topspin serves into either service box. The serve that hits the back fence at the highest point (after landing in the service box) wins.

 High racquet-head speed is essential to generate good spin.

SHORT AND WIDE (2)

For a right-handed server, place some markers on the court to continue the singles sideline, as shown. Play points where, in returning the serve, the receiver is not allowed to put both feet past the singles sideline or the markers.

 The second serve can be transformed into an attacking shot by the use of good placement and spin – in this case, the wide slice serve.

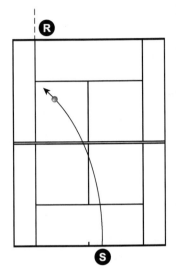

NO ANGLES

For a right-handed server, place some markers on the court to continue the centre service line, as shown. Play points where, in returning the serve, the receiver is not allowed to put both feet past the markers.

 Some receivers can hit great returns if the serve pulls them wide. Here the receiver is forced to the centre of the court and will have to create his own angles.

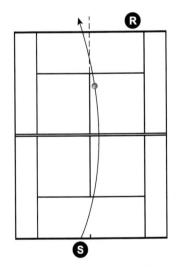

NO MARSHMALLOW SERVES

The server has only one serve per point. The receiver scores two points if he hits a clean winner on the return. The receiver scores one point if the server hits a double fault, i.e. misses one serve.

 Hitting weak second serves that the receiver can blast for a winner is a great way of boosting the receiver's confidence.

ONE AND ONLY

Players play points as normal, but only have one serve per point. All serves are second serves.

 The continental grip must be used in order to put spin on the ball.

DO THE STATS

There is no more objective assessment of the quality of a player's second serve than, 'What does the receiver do with it?' The server hits twenty second serves; count how many times the receiver:
* attacks the second serve;
* defends against the second serve;
* returns with a rallying-type shot;
* fails to return the second serve.

A coach can tell a player that he needs to improve his second serve, but nothing will convince the player more quickly than hard statistics: 'In that exercise the receiver attacked on fifteen of your twenty second serves.'

RETURN OF SERVE

As mentioned earlier, it is generally agreed that the serve is the most important shot in the game. Therefore, the return must be the second-most important, since it is the response to the serve.

- The quality of the return often dictates how the rally will progress.
- The focus is usually on the advantages the server has in a match. However, it is worth bearing in mind that the receiver has the advantage of knowing that the serve must land in an area only slightly larger than 25 per cent of the size of the court.

IN AT THE DEEP END

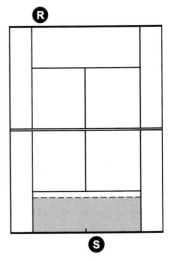

The receiver wins the point if he can bounce his return in the target area (deep). The server wins the point if he does not. How many points can the receiver score from twenty serves?

 This exercise practices returns against a player who is staying back after his serve. The deep return prevents the server from attacking on his second shot, and could force him to hit a short ball which the receiver can attack.

UNDER PRESSURE

The receiver aims for the target area, the opponent's backhand (and generally weaker) side. If the return lands in the target area, play out the point. If not, the server wins the point.

At all levels of tennis, players look to pressurise an opponent's weaknesses. The earlier in the rally you can do this, the better.

TRY TRY AGAIN

Play points as normal, except the receiver has two attempts at every return. If he misses his first return, no point is scored and the server hits his first or second serve again.

 The receiver should be encouraged to take some risks on his return in order to keep the server guessing.

RETURN CC

The receiver is asked to hit all returns crosscourt. The volleyer at the net attempts to intercept and volley into the open court.

 Master the angled crosscourt return in order to pull the server off the court.

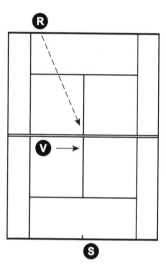

SECOND CHANCES

The server has only one serve per point. If the receiver hits a return that the server cannot get back into play, the receiver scores two points. Otherwise, play on and whoever wins the rally scores one point.

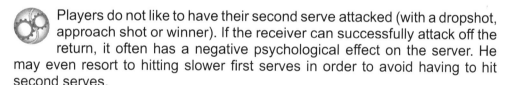 Players do not like to have their second serve attacked (with a dropshot, approach shot or winner). If the receiver can successfully attack off the return, it often has a negative psychological effect on the server. He may even resort to hitting slower first serves in order to avoid having to hit second serves.

COME CLOSER

The serve is hit at full pace from just behind the service line. If the receiver wins the rally, he scores two points. If the server wins the rally, he scores one point.

 One of the keys to returning hard serves, where time is limited, is to use a short backswing.

PLAYING STANDARD: ITN 6-2

Many players find returning serve against the net-rusher to be a nerve-wracking experience. A return that goes high over the net will be quickly put away. The priority is to keep it low, forcing the server to 'volley up'. This will limit the amount of power he can use.

When faced with a serve-volleyer, some returners fall into the trap of thinking that they must win the point with the return. It takes a lot of pressure off the return if, instead, it is used it to 'set up' for winning the rally with the second shot.

TARGET BOUNCE

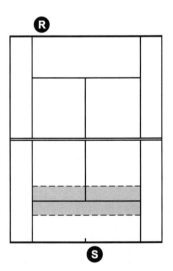

The receiver wins the point if he can bounce the return in the target area. The server wins the point if he does not. How many points can the receiver score from ten serves?

 The target area is where the server's feet will be when he split-steps.

BOUNCE TO WIN

The server serves and volleys. If the return bounces before the server can hit a volley, the receiver wins the point. If not, play out the rally.

The 'dipping' return of serve prevents an attacking first volley.

Use a whipped topspin or a chipped slice shot. The return does not have to be hit at maximum pace to be effective. Some volleyers find it difficult to hit an effective shot off a ball with little pace on it, but will volley well if the incoming shot is fast.

STRETCH THE SERVER

The receiver returns down the line and the volleyer attempts to intercept.

 Down the line is effective because it does not cross the server's bodyline as he moves in for his second shot.

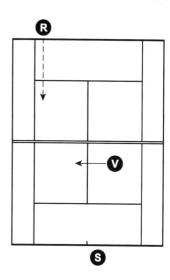

JAM THE SERVER

One player serves and the receiver tries to pass two volleyers.

In singles against a serve-volleyer, hitting the ball low down the middle is good, since it takes the volleyer's angles away.

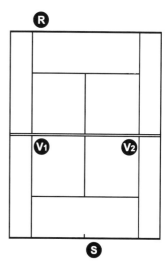

PART TWO:
GROUNDSTROKES

CONSISTENCY 1

All players need to appreciate the huge value of being consistent from the moment they begin to play tennis. If you hit the ball back into play, you cannot lose the point, so it is better to hit it in at one mile per hour than out at one hundred miles per hour.

It is important to stress the concept of 'build-up' in most rallies. It's like fencing with an opponent or pacing yourself in a race. If you return the ball twice, your opponent has two chances to miss; if you hit it back twenty times, he has twenty chances to miss.

LAST LONGEST

Players A and B versus Players C and D, each pair use half of the doubles court. On a signal, both pairs begin to rally. If C and D miss first, A and B score one point. The first pair to score five points wins.

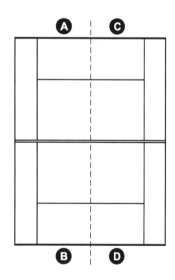

 Aim one to two metres over the net in order to have a good margin for error.

LOWEST WINS

Players rally in pairs for three minutes, counting the number of separate rallies they have. The pair who have had the *lowest* number of rallies wins, since they must have been the most consistent.

 Only hit the ball as hard as you can control it.

BOXING

Players A and B versus Players C and D. Each pair has ten balls in a box. When a pair miss, they start the next rally with a ball from their box. The first pair to run out of balls loses the game.

 Aim one metre inside the lines in order to have a good margin for error.

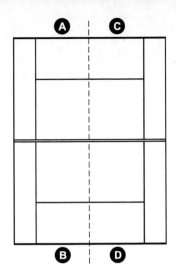

BOXING CLEVER

Players A and B versus Players C and D. Each team has twenty balls in their box. When a pair miss, they start the next rally with a ball from their box. Which team can hit a total of one hundred shots, using the least number of balls from their box?

 Players should be introduced early to the subject of spin and its role in consistency: spin gives control.

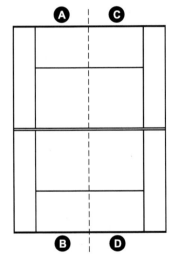

GET BACK

Players A and B rally, while Players C and D wait at opposite back fences. When A and B miss, C and D take a turn to rally. Players will want to stay in, so they will be motivated to play with consistency.

 It is frustrating for an opponent if you are consistent. You can tempt a player to go for a winner from a difficult position, because he gets frustrated when the ball keeps coming back.

IT ALL ADDS UP

Players A and B rally from the baseline. When there is a mistake the player who did not miss adds the number of the rally to his score. For example, there is a rally of twelve shots, then A misses. The score is 12–0 to B. The next rally lasts for twenty shots, then B misses. The score is 20–12 for Player A.

 The longer the rally goes on, the less each player wants to miss. This exercise is useful for putting a player under pressure to be consistent when it really counts.

CONSISTENCY 2

The challenge of playing consistent tennis tests all four areas of a player's game:
- *Technically*, do you have the shots to stay in a long rally?
- *Tactically*, do you select the correct percentage shot as the rally develops?
- *Physically*, do you have the endurance and speed to get to every ball?
- *Mentally*, do you have the concentration and mental toughness to triumph in long rallies?

Always keep in mind that winning slowly is more fun than losing quickly!

TWENTY TO ZERO

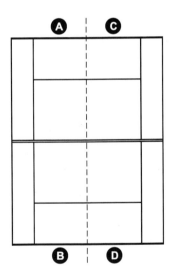

Players A and B are together against C and D. Each pair hits into half a doubles court. On a signal, players start rallying with their partner.

The score is kept by each team counting backwards from twenty, minus one for each shot into court. When a player misses a shot, the team starts again from twenty. The first team to reach zero wins.

 Allowing each pair a full singles court to hit into will make the exercise technically easier and physically harder.

POWER/CONTROL BALANCE

Players A and B are together against C and D. A supply of tennis balls is kept at the back fence. Each rally must start with a ball from the fence. On a signal, players begin rallying with their partner. The first pair to hit a total of two hundred shots into court wins.

 Hitting softly to increase consistency will cost a team 'ball flight time'. Hitting hard to score quickly can result in errors, costing a team time as they collect a new ball from the back fence. This exercise encourages the players to find the correct balance between power and control.

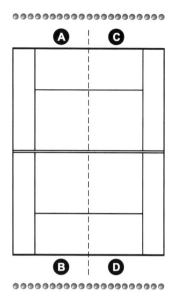

DEEPLY CONSISTENT

Players A and B are together against players C and D. Each pair hits into half a doubles court, but all shots must land deep (past the service line, into the shaded area). On a signal, players start rallying with their partner.

The score is kept by each team counting backwards from twenty, minus one for each shot into the target area. When a player misses a shot, the team adds five to their score (for example twelve becomes seventeen). The first pair to zero wins.

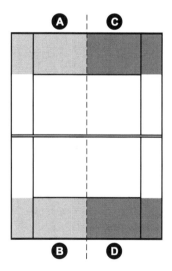

 At a good standard of play, any short shots will be attacked. Players must be able to maintain consistency, while hitting with good depth.

STEADY ON

Two players rally against each other from the baseline. Neither player is allowed to hit a winner or come to the net. Each player tries to win the point by outmaneuvering and outlasting his opponent with consistency and good placement.

 The ability to win points while playing in this fashion gives a player great confidence. He feels that if he can win purely with placement and consistency, he will win very easily when he can bring his attacking shots into the mix.

TEN THEN ATTACK

Two players rally against each other from the baseline, beginning with a drop serve. There must be a rally of ten balls before either player can score. If the rally breaks down before ten shots have been hit, neither player scores.

 Towards the end of the ten shot 'cooperative' rally, players should be encouraged to start to move each other around and off the court, preparing the way to hit a winner as soon as possible after the target of ten has been reached.

DEFENDER V ATTACKER

Two players rally against each other from the baseline, one designated as defender and one as attacker. To win the rally, the defender need only hit six balls in a row back into court. The attacker is forced to go on the offensive, so the defender is practicing consistency against attacking shots.

 A player who can be consistent even when attacked often frustrates his opponent. The attacker is forced to take more and more risks in order to win the point.

GET IT BACK

Two players compete in singles, keeping the score numerically. If one player misses before three shots have been played in the rally, the other player scores three points. If someone misses before five shots have been played (but after three), the opponent scores two points. If one player misses after five or more shots have been played, the opponent scores one point.

 When looking to be consistent, crosscourt is the recommended shot, due to the lower net and the longer (diagonal) court space.

DEPTH 1

PLAYING STANDARD: ITN 10-7

At the beginner stage, a player can win a lot of points simply by keeping the ball in play and deep. At this level, deep can be defined as past the service line, so a ready-made target area exists.

DROP IT

Players drop-feed themselves – five forehands and five backhands. They score one point if the ball is in the singles court and short, and two points if it is in the singles court and deep.

 Height over the net is one of the keys to good depth.

MARK IT

Players drop-feed themselves and try to hit as deep as they can inside the singles court. Their partner on the other end uses a ball to mark the spot where each shot bounces. Discuss which shot lands deepest and why.

 The deeper the better, but players need to keep the 'margin for error' concept in mind.

DOUBLE FOR DEEP

Two players work together, one on each baseline. Player A feeds a ball to Player B, who scores one point if his shot lands short and two points if it lands deep. Change roles after ten shots, with the highest score winning.

 Deep shots help prevent an opponent from attacking.

HIT AND CATCH

One feeder and one hitter form a pair competing against other pairs. They score a point if the feeder can catch a ball hit by his partner after one bounce and without the feeder stepping inside the baseline (or a marker placed further back than the baseline).

 Topspin will make the ball bounce towards the catcher.

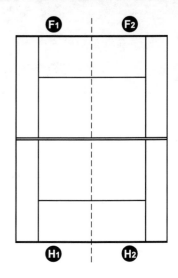

TWENTY DEEP

Rally to twenty, counting only deep shots. How many shots does it take?

 The further back you can keep your opponent, the longer his shot will take to get to you.

PLUS OR MINUS

Two players rally, starting with ten points each. Each *shot* gains or loses one point depending on whether it is deep or short.

 It is important to be able to hit deep shots *consistently*. A player might hit four deep shots in a row, but if the fifth is short it can be attacked, and the four deep shots count for nothing.

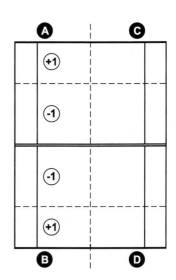

TWO FOR ONE

Two players rally from the baseline. If Player A hits a deep ball and Player B misses, A scores two points and vice versa. If Player A hits a short ball and B misses, A scores one point and vice versa.

 As in any battle, the further away you can keep your enemy the less harm he can do to you.

MAKE HIM VOLLEY

Two players rally, with Player A standing just behind the service line. Player B must hit shots that his partner can volley or the rally ends.

 Players should set themselves a challenging target number of shots that Player B should be able to hit in a row before A has to hit a groundstroke.

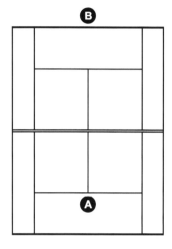

DEPTH 2

PLAYING STANDARD: ITN 6-3

Better players consistently hit the ball very deep into the opponent's court. Two metres inside the baseline now becomes a good target area, since some opponents will attack a ball that lands much shorter than this. Even at the highest levels, it is not necessary to aim to bounce the ball extremely close to the lines; there must still be a margin for error no matter how skilled the player.

PLUS AND MINUS

Player A feeds to Player B. If player B's shot lands in area one, he loses one point. If Player B's shot lands in area two, his score remains the same. If Player B's shot lands in area three, he scores one point. Switch roles after ten attempts, and see who scores the most points.

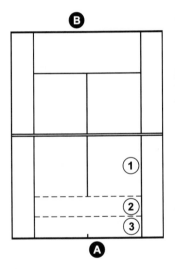

 The further back you can keep your opponent, the less angles are open to him.

ALL DEEP

Players A and B rally. All shots must be deep or the rally ends. With both players cooperating and not going for winners, what is the longest rally they can get from ten balls, or in two minutes?

 The further back you can keep your opponent, the harder it will be for him to get to the net or attack if you do hit short.

DEEP V ANYWHERE

Player A versus Player B. One of the players must hit everything deep or lose the point, but the other player can hit short or deep.

 The further back you can keep an opponent, the more vulnerable he will be to your drop shots.

ALL DEEP POINTS

Players A and B rally. All shots must be deep or the rally ends. Players can attack at any time – there is no cooperative play.

 The further back you can keep an opponent, the greater the distance you can make him run (see diagram).

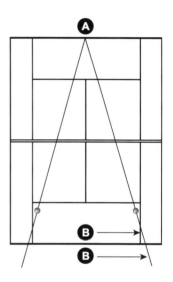

SHORT ATTACK

Player A versus Player B. By hitting deep each player tries to force the other to hit short. The player who gets the first short ball attacks it. Play out the point.

 It can be difficult for an opponent to attack if you are keeping him well back with good depth. However, once you hit short, you are inviting him to attack.

DEEP WINS

If the ball lands very deep (inside the shaded area in the diagram) the player who hit it there wins the point automatically – do not continue the rally.

 Keep in mind the concept of 'margin for error'.

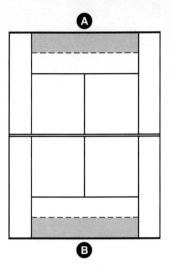

OFF FOR SHORT

Four players rally together from the baseline, using the doubles court. Whoever hits the first short ball quickly moves to the fence, while the rally continues. The remaining three players play out the rally. The team with two players on court must now hit to the half of the doubles court being covered by the solo player.

 Since nobody likes to drop out, all players will be motivated to hit deep.

HITTING EARLY

PLAYING STANDARD: ITN 6-2

Holding your ground and staying near the baseline, rather than being pushed towards the back fence by your opponent's deep shots, has many benefits:

- The earlier you hit the ball, the quicker it reaches your opponent;
- You will be quicker to attack a short ball;
- Your opponent's shots cannot pull you as wide;
- You will be able to hit more widely angled shots;
- You will be hitting a higher ball;
- It sends a message to your opponent about your attacking intentions.

MOVE AND CATCH

Two players throw the ball to each other overarm, baseline to baseline. Practice the footwork needed to get into position to catch the ball while rising or at the peak of the bounce.

 Split step as the thrower releases the ball.

RISING BALL

Players rally in the service boxes, contacting the ball 'on the rise' (while it is still rising upwards after the bounce).

 Use an early, short backswing.

CLIFFHANGER

Players rally from the back of the court. One or both players must stay just inside the baseline, no backing-off allowed. Imagine there is a ten-metre cliff behind the baseline!

 A short backswing combined with a firm wrist will make the timing easier.

EARLY PASS

Player A feeds to Player B, who hits a short ball. A plays an approach shot. B hits the passing shot early, and they play out the point.

 Taking the passing shot early means that the volleyer is further back, so it will be more difficult for him to play an attacking volley.

RETURN EARLY

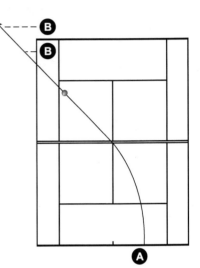

Player A hits wide slice serves (to the deuce court if he is right handed). Player B focuses on taking the return early.

 Returning early means B is not pulled as wide off the court as he would be if he stayed back to return this type of serve.

EARLY APPROACH

Player A feeds to Player B, who hits a short ball. Player A plays the approach on the rise and they play out the point.

 The earlier the approach is hit the easier it will be to get to the volley position, since the early approach will have been played from closer to the net.

STAY IN

Play sets in singles or doubles where all players must stay inside the sidelines and baselines at all times (except the server, when he is serving).

As well as working on hitting the ball early, this exercise encourages players to hit angled shots, since they can win the rally by making the opponent put a foot past the sideline.

ACCURACY

It is of course fundamental for a player to be able to hit the ball where he wants it to go. The primary target at any level is always into court. However, at a very early stage in a player's development, there should be a focus on hitting away from the opponent and directing the majority of shots to his weaker side.

TRAMLINES DL

Players A and B rally down the line, aiming to bounce their shots between the singles and doubles sideline.

 The ball will go wherever the racquet is pointing when contact is made.

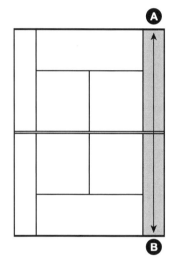

TRAMLINES CC

Players A and B rally crosscourt, aiming to bounce their shots between the opposite singles and doubles sidelines.

 'Point of contact' is crucial for accuracy. In general, the earlier the contact between racquet and ball, the more angle crosscourt will be achieved. With later contact, the shot will travel more down the line.

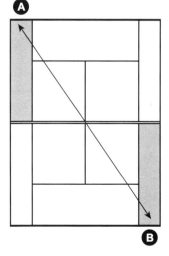

ALTERNATE SIDES

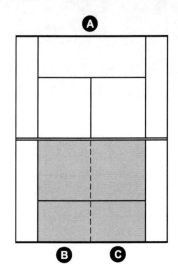

Player A hits alternately to Player B and C's side of the court. How many in a row can he achieve?

A tired opponent makes more mistakes than a fresh opponent.

THREE CHOICES

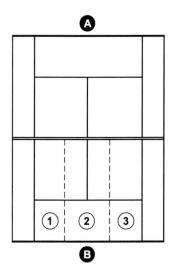

Player A hits alternately to areas one, two and three. As a progression, the coach can call out which area he wants the player to hit to. Finally, this decision can be left to the player.

The third progression of this exercise provides an opportunity for a coach to discover which area his player favours – does he select the correct spot tactically or is there an area he avoids hitting to because he is not confident he can hit that target?

TARGET WINS

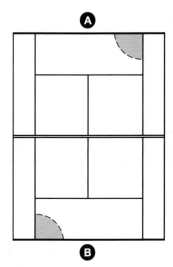

Players A and B rally. If either player's shot lands in their target area, the player who hit the target automatically wins the point.

Deep to an opponent's backhand is a very effective shot against almost all players.

WIDE PASS

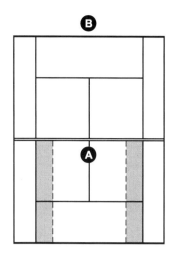

Player A volleys and Player B hits passing shots. Player B scores two points if his shot is heading for the target area and Player A cannot return it, and one point if he wins the point in any other way.

 A well-placed passing shot at medium pace can be more effective than a hard-hit shot that is near the volleyer.

CLEAN WINNERS

Two players rally, keeping the score numerically. If either player hits a clean winner (a shot that the opponent cannot touch at all or until after the ball has bounced twice), he scores two points instead of one.

 Hitting clean winners in a match can have a negative psychological effect on an opponent.

TOUCH WINS

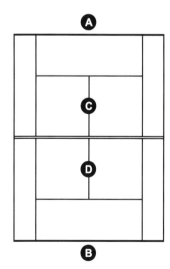

Players A and B rally (no lobs allowed), while Players C and D sit on the court. If Players C or D can touch their opponent's shot with their racquet, they win the point for their team.

The emphasis here is on control rather than power, and these are good watchwords for the recreational-level player.

PART THREE:
NET PLAY

APPROACHING THE NET 1

PLAYING STANDARD: ITN 10-8

Starter and recreational-level players are often reluctant to approach the net. Understanding the advantages of being there can help convince them that net play is a set of skills worth mastering:

- The player at the net can hit wider angles;
- A volley gives an opponent less time to react than a shot hit from the baseline;
- When faced with an opponent at the net, many players feel under pressure, which can lead to errors.

When it comes to the approach shot, it is important for players to understand that its purpose is not to win the point, but to pave the way for a successful volley.

SERVICE-LINE SERVE

Player A serves from the service line, moves in and volleys.

 A difficult serve to return, combined with a short distance for the volleyer to move, allows the volleyer to experience success.

MANY HANDS...

The player stands at the baseline near the coach, who serves. As the coach hits the serve, the player moves forward to continue the rally by 'serving and volleying'.

 The coach controls the serve in such a way as to set up a comfortable first volley for the player.

DROP APPROACH

The coach drops a ball from his hand onto the service line. Player A moves forward, plays an approach shot and the point is played out in a half court.

 Player A should ensure that he performs a split step as his opponent is about to contact the ball.

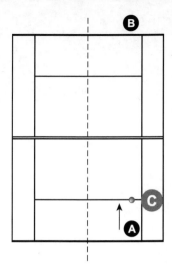

COVER ME

Player A approaches the net off a short ball hit by Player B. The coach stays at the baseline and returns any shot that A cannot reach.

 The 'safety net' of having the coach at the baseline encourages Player A to experiment.

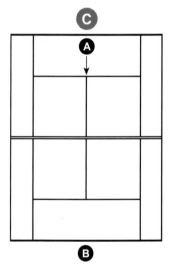

BOTH SIDES NOW

Standing near the net, the coach feeds a short ball to Player A, who approaches and plays out the point with Player B. While the next two players (D and E) have their rally, A and B change ends (and roles).

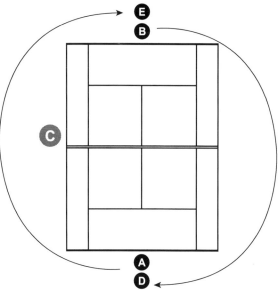

 Alternating volleys and passes helps develop an understanding of: what is a good approach shot, and the pressure on the passing shot player.

RISKS AND REWARDS

Play a set as normal, but if either player wins the point with a volley or smash, he wins the game. For example, if the score is 15-all and Player A wins the third point with a volley, it is game to Player A.

 Approaching the net is riskier than staying at the baseline, and in tennis risk-taking should be rewarded.

PLAYING STANDARD: ITN 7-5

One of the distinguishing features of the intermediate-level player is that he begins to feel more and more comfortable at the net. Even for a committed baseliner, it is important to be able to charge the net occasionally for variety. The ability to approach and play from the net position is crucial for successful doubles play.

COACH APPROACH 1

Player A feeds a ball to the coach, who volleys a short ball in return. Player A then plays an approach shot and plays out the point in a half court with Player B (no lobs allowed).

 Approaching off a ball controlled by the coach in a half court and without the danger of being lobbed helps the volleyer build confidence.

Approaching off short balls in a match forces the opponent to try to hit deeper to prevent this happening – taking him out of his comfort zone.

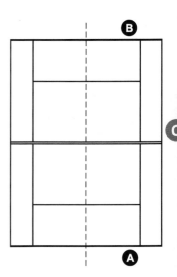

COACH APPROACH 2

The coach hits a weak second serve. Player A plays his return of serve down the line, as an approach shot, and then plays out the point with Player B in a half court (no lobs allowed).

 Approaching off a serve controlled by the coach in a half court and without the danger of being lobbed encourages the receiver to pressurise the server by moving in to the net.

Hitting the approach down the line is the correct decision in most cases.

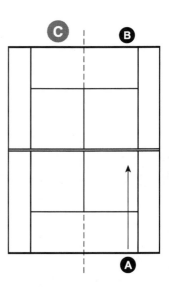

MUST S&V

Two players play points where the server must always serve and volley. However, the server can keep hitting first serves until he gets it in. If he misses a first serve, he has another one and so on.

 A good first serve paves the way for an easy volley.

The server must move forward without hesitation, before he even knows if the serve will be in or out.

OVER AND IN

Player A starts at the baseline and Player B is close to the net. B feeds to A, who plays a lob. Player B retreats to the baseline to retrieve the lob with a forehand or backhand. As B moves back, Player A moves to the net. Play out the point.

 Moving to the net position when your lob has sent the opponent scurrying back is a good move tactically, because it puts pressure on your opponent to play a good shot.

TWO FOR ONE

Players A and B play a set. Either player scores two points if they win the rally with a volley or smash and one point for winning with any other shot.

 This exercise helps players integrate the main methods of approaching the net into their normal singles game.

MUST APPROACH

Players A and B rally from the baseline. If a ball lands inside the service line, the player who receives it must play an approach shot and go to the net.

 If approaching on the backhand side, slice is useful in order to keep the ball low.

RETURN AND IN

The server hits only second serves. If the serve lands in area x, the receiver must play his return of serve as an approach shot and go to the net.

 Pressurising an opponent's second serve in this way can cause him to ease up on his first serve in order to stop you attacking his second serve.

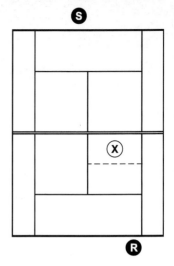

NARROW REWARD

Two players play points. For baseline rallies, the full singles court is used. However, if either player comes to the net, the other player has to hit inside the drop-down lines or the ball is wide.

This exercise simultaneously rewards the player who approaches and makes it easier for him to win the point from the net.

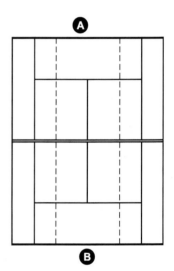

NO PRESSURE APPROACH

Two players play points. If a shot lands inside the service line during a rally, the player who receives it calls 'short' and automatically wins the point. However, that player must approach the net and the rally is played out for practice.

 Players must feel free to experiment in practice. In this exercise the player approaching the net has already won the point, so there is no pressure.

PLAYING STANDARD: ITN 4-1

An advanced player will often find himself under pressure at the net, due to the quality of his opponent's passing shots and lobs. In order to prepare for this, the exercises in this session pile pressure onto the player who is approaching the net.

MUST VOLLEY

Players A and B start a rally from the baseline, playing in a half court. Player A starts by feeding the ball in to his opponent, then A moves to the net position. If Player B's shot bounces on A's side, A loses the point – the net player must volley everything.

 The emphasis is simply on quick forward movement.

BOTH MUST VOLLEY

Players A and B start a rally from the baseline, playing in a half court. Player A starts by feeding a ball to his opponent, which must land around the service-line area. Player A moves to the net, while his opponent has to take his first shot early and also move to the net. If either player lets the ball bounce on their side (except for the feed-in ball), they lose the point.

 Volley to volley is unusual in singles, but central in doubles.

ONE BOUNCE ONLY

Play a set on the full singles court, where each player can only allow the ball to bounce once on his side of the net in each rally (excluding the return of serve).

 Vary the rules by specifying that the server must serve and volley; the server is not allowed to serve and volley; the server has one or two serves; the server must serve underarm.

VOLLEY SET

Play a set in the full singles court where the ball is not allowed to bounce, except on return of serve. Allow only one serve per point, to give the receiver a chance to get in to the net position.

 In a set played under these rules, both players will often find themselves in awkward positions, with difficult volleys to play. This experience will pay dividends when it comes to real matchplay.

VOLLEY V TWO

Using the singles court, Players A and B compete against Player C in a 'two versus one' set up. Player C feeds to A, who returns a short ball allowing C to play an approach shot. Player C moves to the net and plays out the point against two opponents.

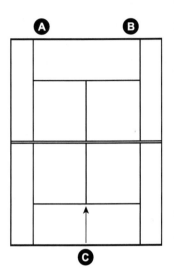

 This type of 'overload training' toughens up the net player.

CLEAN WINNERS ONLY

Player A starts at the service line and feeds a ball to Player B before closing in to the net. Player B must hit his first shot towards his opponent, then they play out the point. To score, Player A must hit a clean winner. If B gets his racquet to the ball, A does not score.

 The volleyer is encouraged to hit angled volleys. From the net position, short angled shots are more effective than deep shots.

VOLLEY THE SERVE

The receiver stands half-way between the service line and the baseline. As the server releases his toss, the receiver moves forward into the service box. He must volley or half volley the serve and then play out the point. To make it even tougher for the receiver, the server can be asked to serve and volley.

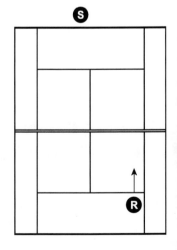

 Controlling the volley against such an extreme 'passing shot' requires a very firm wrist.

THE VOLLEY 1

The net is where most beginners least like to be, despite the fact that the volley is the simplest shot in tennis. When compared to groundstrokes, there is less emphasis on grip change and less swing. Furthermore, it is easier to judge the trajectory of a ball that does not bounce. So there is every reason to expose young players to net play right from the start of their development.

NET V BASELINE

Players A and B are on their baselines. Player A has ten balls lined up and attempts to hit as many winning shots as he can after drop-feeding to himself. Player B tries to return the shots. Repeat the exercise, this time with Player A at the net position.

 It is inevitable that more winners will be hit from the net due to the greater possibilities to hit angled shots. This exercise is a practical way of selling the idea that players should develop their skills at the net.

THROW AND CATCH

Two players stand near the net and throw the ball to each other. Progress to one player volleying with the palm of his hand.

 The player catching will automatically use a volley-type motion, i.e. no swing.

Step forward as you contact the ball.

IN OR NOT?

Two (or four) players rally by throwing the ball across the net, aiming to keep it inside the service boxes while moving the opponent around. If either player can catch the ball before it bounces, he wins the rally and scores one point.

 This exercise helps players discover when it is wise to move forward and when it is better to stay back.

THROW AND VOLLEY

Thrower tosses to volleyer, who may shorten his grip on the racquet if necessary.

 An opportunity to emphasise the firm wrist: *you don't kick a ball by flicking your ankle; why volley it by flicking your wrist?*

HANDLE VOLLEY

Thrower tosses to volleyer, who volleys the ball back with the handle of his racquet, rather than with the strings.

 This exercise discourages swinging, since the 'racquet face' is only a few centimetres wide.

FENCED IN

The volleyer stands with his back to the fence. His partner throws balls for him to volley.

 The volleyer cannot use a backswing because the fence is in the way. This mirrors how he should play the volley when on court.

TEAM CATCH

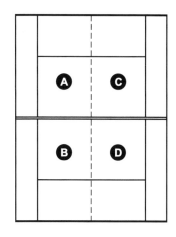

Players A and B versus Players C and D. A throws to B. Player B volleys so that A can catch the ball. If A does catch the ball, he scores a point for his team. First team to ten points wins.

 Control of direction is crucial for successful volleying.

VOLLEY 2 VOLLEY

Players A and B versus Players C and D. All players are at the volleying position near the net. On a signal, each pair begins a volley rally. When one pair misses, the other pair (who are still volley rallying) scores a point. First team to ten points wins.

 Volley-to-volley rallies emphasise how little time there is to swing the racquet when playing from the net.

NO BOUNCE

Two players rally in two of the service boxes. Only the serve is allowed to bounce. If the ball bounces in the service box, the point is lost by the player on whose side it bounced.

 This is a very useful exercise for developing the touch that is vital for successful net play.

PASS V VOLLEY

Player A is in the volleying position, Player B is at the baseline, and they play in half the width of the doubles court. A feeds to B, who attempts a pass. If Player A volleys the ball back into court, he scores one point (do not play on the rally). See how many points A can score from ten balls; then switch roles.

 In singles if one player comes to the net, the other usually stays back.

THE VOLLEY 2

While tennis has become in recent years a game mostly played from the baseline, it can be very useful in certain situations to be able to take control of the net:

- If a player is losing a match from the baseline, moving forward follows the principle of 'always change a losing game'.
- If a singles opponent is having success by approaching the net, you can take the initiative away from him by getting to the volley position before he does.
- If competing on a fast surface such as grass, playing a net game avoids tricky bounces, while giving an opponent less time to play his shots.
- Although most singles matches are now baseline-to-baseline encounters, doubles remains a game where getting to the net equals a better chance of success.

HALF COURT PASS

Player A is in the volleying position and Player B is at the baseline. They play in half the width of the doubles court. Player A feeds in a ball to his opponent and they play out the rally using passing shots and volleys.

Using a half court means longer rallies, and it simulates doubles situations.

NET GAINS

Players A and B rally from the baseline, playing in half the width of the doubles court. Whoever wins the baseline rally comes to the net and starts the next rally from there. If the player at the net wins the next rally, he scores a point and stays in the volleying position. If the player at the net loses the rally, he moves to the baseline and his opponent becomes the volleyer. Only the player at the net can score points.

Since only the player at the net can score, this exercise puts a positive slant on being in the volleying position.

The exercise can also be used for four players in a doubles situation, using the full doubles court.

SIDE TO SIDE

Player A, volleying against Players B and C, must hit to alternate sides of the court or he loses the point.

 From the net, move the baseliner side to side.

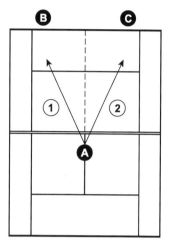

SIDE AND WIDE

Player A feeds a ball to Player B, who returns the feed down the middle, following which they play out the point. For the rest of the rally Player A must keep his shots out of the central lane or he loses the point.

 The ability to hit angles is one of the big advantages of being at the net.

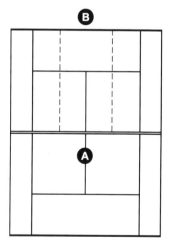

CHAMPIONS AND CHALLENGERS

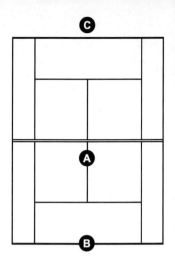

The volleyers (Players A and B) are the challengers, the player at the baseline (Player C) is the champion. Player B awaits his turn, while A feeds in a ball to Player C, who aims his first shot down the middle of the court and they play out the rally. If the volleyer wins the rally, he stays on and has another rally. If he wins the second rally he becomes the new champion. Only the champion can score points.

 A player who is winning groups of points from the net position puts his opponent under pressure to keep him at the baseline.

STRAIGHT DOUBLES

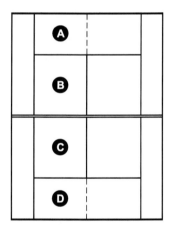

Players A and B versus Players C and D, playing in half the width of the doubles court. The two back-court players are not allowed inside the service line. The two net players are not allowed behind the service line. No bounces – all shots must be volleys or the point is over.

A good opportunity for the back-court players to practice the lob volley – a useful doubles shot.

For safety reasons, the players at the net position are not allowed to smash even if they can reach the lob volley.

THE DROP VOLLEY

This shot is all about absorbing pace. Much of the speed of the incoming ball has to be taken off it in order for a drop volley to be successful. This is achieved by moving the racquet head in the same direction as the ball is travelling, i.e. towards the back fence.

KILL IT 1

Player throws a ball straight up in the air and catches it on his racquet strings, without letting the ball bounce off the strings.

 In order for the ball not to bounce off the strings, the racquet must travel in the same direction as the ball – in this case downwards.

KILL IT 2

Player A throws a ball to Player B from three or four metres away. Player B 'kills it' on his strings.

 This exercise is a progression of the one above, but this time the ball is coming at the volleyer, as it would in a game situation.

UP AND CATCH

Player A is at the baseline, Player B at the net. A feeds a ball to B, who hits the ball up in the air and then catches it with his free hand. The less Player B has to move between hitting and catching, the more control he has.

 The racquet acts like a crumple zone in a car: it moves in the same direction as the force of the impact in order to absorb the force.

THE ART GAME

Players play singles in two service boxes (or doubles in four boxes) with no bounces allowed. This encourages each player to drop the ball short in front of their opponent.

 While hitting the ball hard is a skill, some believe that hitting it gently is an art.

VOLLEYBALL TENNIS

Play doubles in the four service boxes using a volleyball format – players can keep the ball on their side by hitting soft volleys to each other until they are ready to hit over the net. Each time the ball crosses the net, it is allowed to bounce *once* before it is hit back.

 In this exercise, multiple 'touch' volleys are played in a short period of time.

The game can also be played with three or four players per team.

CAN IT

Players work in threes against other teams of three. Player A hits a ball with pace to Player B, who plays a drop volley. For their team to score a point, Player C must catch the ball in a tennis ball can or tin he is holding, before it bounces.

 Another option in this exercise is that Player C cannot step back further than the line of markers and the ball must bounce once before he catches it.

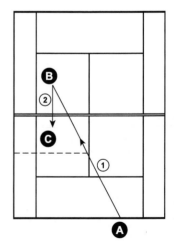

KEEP IT SHORT

The coach feeds a ball to Player A, who plays a drop volley. For his team to score, Player A must hit a ball into court that the opponents (Players C and D) cannot catch until it has bounced more than once. The catching team are not allowed to step inside the service line.

 A good drop volley should bounce several times before it reaches the service line.

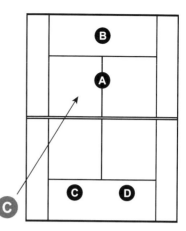

PART FOUR:
THE EXTRAS

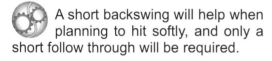

THE DROP SHOT

The drop shot can be used to tire an opponent, to vary the rhythm of play and to bring a baseliner in to the net. Perhaps the most common error made on the shot is to attempt to hit it with a lot of underspin. To get heavy slice you must swing, and swinging gives you too much power. The key is to focus on hitting the ball gently, as if playing with a small child.

PYRAMID GAME

Players A and B rally from near the service line. They try to knock down their opponent's 'pyramid' of four balls, which have been placed about two metres from the net.

 A short backswing will help when planning to hit softly, and only a short follow through will be required.

INSIDE THE LINE

Mark a line two metres from the net. Player A feeds a short ball to his partner, who plays a drop shot. If the drop shot bounces inside the line, Player B scores one point. See how many points he can score out of ten feeds; then change roles.

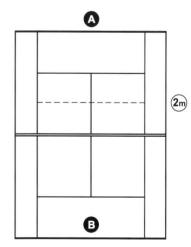

'You are playing with your six-year-old cousin!'

BOUNCE CATCH

Players A and B versus Players C and D. Player A feeds a ball to his partner and B attempts to hit a shot that A can catch *after* it bounces once. Player A must stay inside the line of markers. The first pair to score ten points wins.

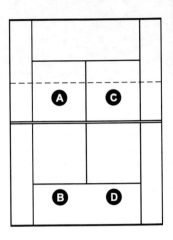

 The emphasis is on 'soft hands'.

BRING THEM IN

Four players play doubles in the four service boxes. All shots must be allowed to bounce. When a team wins a point, they serve by dropping the ball off the net cord. Soft shots only – no powerful shots allowed.

 Using good touch play, bring the opponents forward and make them volley – if they volley, they lose the point.

FREEZE

Player A stands two metres behind the baseline and feeds a short ball to Player B, who plays a drop shot. Player A cannot move until the drop shot has been hit; then the point is played out.

 A good drop shot will bounce two to three times before crossing the service line.

IN DISGUISE

Player A stands behind the baseline and feeds a series of short balls to Player B, who can choose to play a drop shot, an approach shot or a winner. Play out the rallies.

Player B is encouraged to disguise his intention by preparing for the shot in a similar manner, no matter which of the three shots he intends to play.

YOUR CHOICE

Players A and B rally from the baseline, each trying to force his opponent to hit a short ball. Whoever receives the first short ball moves forward and hits a drop shot, an approach shot or a winner. A winning drop shot scores three points; winning the rally with any other shot scores one point.

Drop shots are played off short balls; the best way to get a short ball is to hit deep.

Playing a drop shot off a deep ball is difficult; even if you play it well, the opponent has lots of time to see it and move in (it is a soft shot travelling a long distance).

THE HALF VOLLEY

The half volley can be a difficult shot to practice, since it demands very precise feeding. It is one situation where it is useful to have a ball machine, which can be programmed to bounce the ball on the same spot time after time. In a match the half volley is best avoided whenever possible. However, since it cannot always be avoided, practices must be set up to allow a player to master the shot.

MUST HALF VOLLEY

Players A and B rally at a slow pace, both players starting at their service line. By moving backwards and forwards, each player must try to play a half volley off every ball they receive.

 This exercise is also useful in the later stages of a warm up.

HALF VOLLEY TARGETS

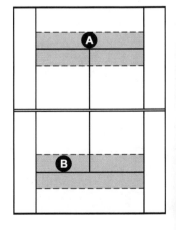

Both players stay inside their shaded area and aim all their shots to land in their partner's shaded area.

 Most half volleys are played from these areas.

Players should bend at the knees, rather than drop the racquet head or bend their backs.

SERVE FEED

One player hits gentle serves from the service line, aiming for the opposite service line. The receiver tries to play a half-volley return and then they play out the point.

 The serve is the most effective shot for feeding the half volley.

DEEP HALF VOLLEY

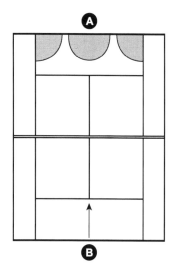

Players A and B start at their baselines. As Player A feeds in a ball (aiming for the service line), Player B moves forward and plays a half volley aiming for the target areas. Only play out the point if the half volley lands in one of the target areas.

 As half volleys are hit upwards, they cannot be hit hard or they will go long.

Good depth is necessary to make up for the lack of pace.

HALF VOLLEY RETURN

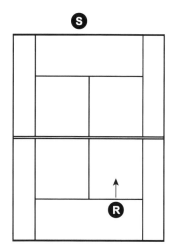

The server hits normal-paced serves from the baseline, aiming for the opposite service line. The receiver starts half-way between the service line and the baseline, then moves forward as the server tosses up the ball. The receiver tries to play a half volley return of serve and then they play out the point.

 It puts extra demands on each player if the server is requested to always serve and volley.

THE LOB

In recreational-level tennis, the lob is a very effective shot in both singles and doubles. While the length and width of the court are restricted, in outdoor play height above the court is unlimited.

FIVE, THREE, ONE

Player A is at the baseline and Player B is at the net. Player A self-feeds and hits ten lobs, which B attempts to smash. Player B is not allowed to go behind the service line. Player A scores:
- Five points if B cannot touch the ball;
- Three points if B hits it but cannot get it back;
- One point if B returns it but A goes on to win the rally.

Change roles and compare scores.

 High, short lobs are ineffective – good depth is important.

TEAM LOB

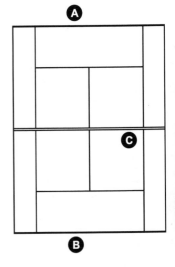

Players A, B and C are together as a team, competing against other teams of three players. Player C feeds a ball to A who plays a high, deep lob. To score a point for his team, Player B must catch the ball (in his hand or in a ball can) after one bounce without coming inside the baseline. The first team to score ten points wins. Then players rotate positions.

 If a lob gets over an opponent's head and has good depth, it is likely to be a winner.

PLUS OR MINUS

The court is marked as shown in the diagram. Player B feeds balls to Player A, who lobs, scoring or losing points depending on where the ball bounces. How many points can A score from ten balls, or how many balls does it take for him to score thirty points?

 Deep to the backhand side scores most, since the backhand smash is generally regarded as the most difficult shot in tennis.

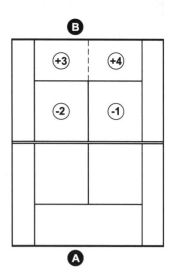

TIP TO WIN

Players A and B are together versus Players C and D. Players A and B play only lobs. Players C and D cannot move behind the service line. C and D score one point if A and B hit out, or if they tip with their racquet any of the lobs from A and B. Players A and B win the rally if they can hit eight consecutive lobs into the court that their opponents cannot touch. See how many points Players C and D can score from twenty rallies; then change roles.

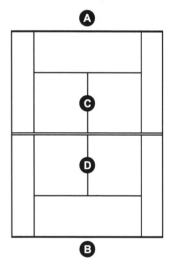

For safety reasons, no smashes are allowed in this exercise. Players at the net need only make contact with the lob to win the point.

A lob may be going deep, but not high enough to get over the net player. This exercise emphasises height *and* depth.

THE SMASH

The smash is a 'confidence shot': if you think you will miss it, you probably will. Self-belief is vital. Time can appear to stand still as the lob descends to your hitting zone, allowing you plenty of opportunity to worry about what is going to happen next. If players are introduced to the smash sooner rather than later, it helps them to develop long-term confidence in the shot. By doing so we can help to avoid the problem that the player who *cannot* smash *will not* volley.

CATCH THE LOB

Player A is at the net and Player B is at the baseline. Player A feeds a ball to B, who plays a lob. Player A *catches* the ball in his racquet hand, arm outstretched.

Moving the correct way to the correct position on court is a central requirement for a successful smash.

AFTER THE BOUNCE

Player A is at the net; B is at the baseline. Player A feeds a ball to B, who hits a steep, short lob, aiming for the service line. Player A lets the ball bounce before smashing it.

The lob will be travelling slower after the bounce, so the player smashing should experience more success.

GO FOR IT

Player A is at the net and Player B is at the baseline. Player A feeds a ball to B, who lobs. Player A scores:

- Five points for a clean winner smash;
- Three points if B touches the smash but does not get it back;
- One point if B gets the smash back into play, but A goes on to win the rally.

See how many points A can score from ten balls; then change roles.

 The serve and the smash are similar. However, at this level, the serve is designed to put the ball into play, but the smash is designed to put it out of play.

LOB X 3

Players B, C and D lob. Player A will get a lot of practice on the smash, since many smashes will come back.

 The angled smash can be a winner here – even on this power shot, placement has an important role to play.

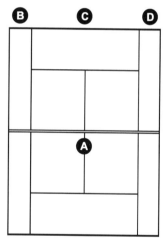

LOB AND SMASH

It makes perfect sense to work on these two shots together, since the smash is the answer to the question asked by the lob. For the advanced player, one of the main uses of the lob is that its 'threat' prevents the volleyer getting too close to the net. This in turn opens up possibilities for angled, low passing shots. Never using the lob means more effective volleys from your opponent.

LINE OF THREE

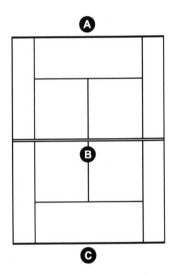

Player C starts each rally by feeding a ball to Player A, who lobs. Player B smashes, while C retrieves anything B cannot reach and keeps the rally going.

 Player B should be encouraged to allow Player C as few shots as possible, and a scoring system could be built around this: B scores two points if he wins a rally, but he scores only one point if C has played two or more shots in the rally. Change roles after twenty rallies and see which player scores most points from the net position.

ANGLE THE SMASH

Player A lobs and B smashes. Player B scores:
- No points if A returns the smash;
- One point if A gets his racquet to the ball but cannot return it;
- Two points if the ball hits the back fence without A touching it;
- Three points if the ball hits the side fence without A touching it.

See how many points B can score from twenty feeds; then change roles.

 A short, angled smash is generally better than a deep smash, since it stays further away from the player who has hit the lob.

MUST LOB

Players A and B rally from the baseline. Whoever gets a short ball approaches and the other player must lob – no passing shots are allowed.

 This exercise reverses the normal order, where the passing shot is the first choice and so guarantees lots of lob and smash practice.

DOUBLE YOUR SCORE

Play points in singles or doubles format. A winning lob or smash scores two points; winning the rally with any other shot scores one point.

 Players should *welcome* the opportunity to smash, since it is one of the shots hit with most pace.

On the smash, your target is almost four times as big as on the serve and you are closer to the target.

PART FIVE:
DOUBLES PLAY

POSITIONING – THE BASICS

PLAYING STANDARD: ITN 10-7

Over a period of many years, basic doubles positions for the start of a point have evolved. These are the positions that give players the best possibility of winning the point.

SHOW ME

The coach stands in position to receive serve in doubles. He asks the players to stand where they think they should be if they were his partner. Discussions and explanations follow. Play some points with the emphasis on the receiver's partner being in the correct position. Repeat the exercise for the other three positions.

Players may be pulled out of position during a rally. However, there is no excuse for being in the wrong place at the start of a point, when there is time to get it right.

YOU LOSE...

Play doubles points. If the coach sees a player out of position just before the serve is hit, he awards the point to the other team.

The main purpose of the 'correct' positions is to give the opponents the smallest possible spaces to hit to.

FREEZE

Play doubles points. Rather than the coach spotting that a player is out of position just before the serve is hit, the opponents must observe it. When a player thinks he sees someone standing in a bad position, he calls 'Stop!' and all players freeze. If the coach decides that the player in question is out of position, he awards the point to the opposing team.

 This exercise encourages players to look at what is happening on the other side of the net.

GO FOR IT

Play doubles points. Players observe the opponents' positions and take advantage by hitting to any openings caused by poor positioning.

 Learn to adapt your play to take advantage of opponents' weaknesses.

SERVING

PLAYING STANDARD: ITN 7-4

Serving in doubles differs from serving in singles. In doubles, the emphasis is on getting a high percentage of first deliveries into play. This encourages the serve and volley tactic, while making it more difficult for the receiver to pressurize the server's partner with the return.

STICK IT

Each of the four players serves three games each. When a server misses a first serve, he sticks a ball in the back fence (after the point ends). The coach or one of the other players keeps track of how many points are played in each game. At the end of the games, the server can easily work out his percentage of first serves in.

 Many players have no idea of the amount of first serves they are missing. They are often surprised to see how many balls are in the back fence at the end of a few service games.

ONLY TWO

Play a set of doubles where the server has only two second serves per game. Once he has used the two second serves allocated to that game, he must get all his first serves in or it is a double fault.

 Add some spin to the serve in order to get a high percentage into play. Spin automatically takes some speed off the shot.

SPIN IT IN

Play a set of doubles where the server has only one serve per point. This should not cause major problems to the serving team, since getting a high percentage of first serves in is standard practice in good level doubles.

 In attempting to ensure that the serve goes in, many intermediate level players slow down the racquet head. The real solution is to speed up the swing, while brushing up and across the ball. This generates spin, which in turn gives more control.

TWO FOR ONE

Play a set of doubles where the serving team scores two points if they win the rally after getting the first serve in. If they win the rally after a second serve, they score one point.

 At a good level of doubles, the server looks to get about 80 per cent of first serves into play.

MY SERVE

Play doubles points using numerical point scoring (for example 2–1 instead of 30–15). One player serves until he misses his first serve. The point is played out on a second serve. Then the player on the opposing team whose turn it is serves, until he misses his first serve.

 Keep track of which of the four players serves the highest number of points in a row.

LOVE SERVE

Play doubles points using numerical scoring. The server continues to serve until his team loses a point; then the opponents serve.

 The holy grail in this exercise is for the server to win four points in a row. In a match, this would equate to holding serve to love.

WHERE TO?

Play a set in which, before the server begins the point, he must tell his partner where he intends to place the serve ('wide', 'body', 'middle').

 As well as encouraging communication between partners, this exercise forces the server to make a decision about what he intends to do with the serve.

COMEBACK

Play a set of doubles where the serving team starts each game at 0–30. The challenge is for the serving team to come back and win the game from this situation.

 If the serving team can win some games from this situation, the exercise serves as a great confidence builder.

If they are struggling to win games, it is an opportunity for them to discover what they need to change in order to be successful when coming back from behind.

RECEIVING SERVE

In doubles, a good return of serve is crucial. The server's partner can easily hit a winner off a weak return. With the possibility of both opponents being at the net to attack, the return must be a quality shot.

GET IT BACK

Play doubles points using numerical scoring. The serving team scores three points if the receiving team fails to return the serve into play.

 The focus is on the receiver to get the ball back into play at all costs.

USE THE WIDTH

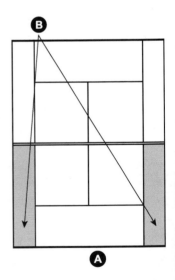

Player A serves to Player B, whose return must land in either tramline for him to score a point. See how many points B can score from twenty serves; then switch roles.

 Accuracy and low over the net are more important than power.

The down-the-line return is very effective if the serving team is using the Australian formation.

TOUCH IT

Play doubles points using normal scoring. The serving team wins the point if the server's partner can touch the return of serve with his racquet (he does not have to hit it back into play).

Progress to a situation where the serving team wins the point if the server's partner can volley the return of serve back into court (he does not have to hit a winning shot).

 The receiver must keep the ball away from the server's partner, who is in the dominant position at the net.

MAKE IT BOUNCE

Play doubles points using normal scoring. The receiver returns crosscourt and low. If he can bounce the ball in front of the serve-volleyer (i.e the server has to play a half volley or groundstroke), the receiving team wins the point.

 The low crosscourt shot is the most important return of serve option in doubles.

This exercise also works on encouraging the server to move quickly to the net position.

PRESSURE RETURN

The coach serves and the receiver must attempt to pass two volleyers. Play out the point with the volleyers always hitting to the receiver's half of the court (shaded area).

This piles the pressure on the receiver. It is even more difficult than returning against a serve-volley team, because both opponents are already established at the net.

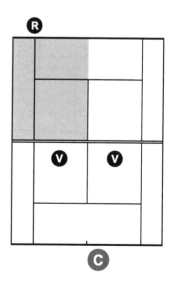

NET PLAY

When both members of a doubles team are at the net they are hard to pass, since each player only has to cover a relatively narrow court. Getting to the net is the essential doubles strategy. It puts pressure on the opposition, because they know that their shot will be volleyed for a winner unless it is of high quality.

GO

Players A and B rally crosscourt from the baseline. Players C and D intercept when they think the time is right.

If a net player moves too soon, the baseliner can go down the line. The volleyer must wait until the baseliner is committed to hitting crosscourt.

A possible variation in this exercise is that the two net players are together against the two baseliners.

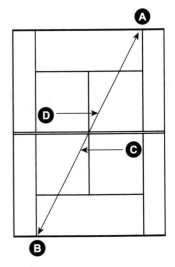

GET IN

Player A feeds the ball to Players C or D, who try to 'fence' their way into the net. If C and D are both inside the service line when the rally ends, and they win it, they score two points. Players C and D score one point if either is still behind the service line when they win the rally.

While two at the net is unusual in singles, four at the net is common in doubles.

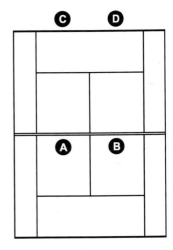

TWO GO IN

Players A and B versus Players C and D. All players begin at the baseline. Player A feeds in the first ball from the baseline; then A and B both rush to the net and must not allow the ball to bounce on their side of the court for the rest of the rally.

 Good net coverage in doubles demands *both* members of a team are together at the volleying position.

FOUR GO IN

Four players rally from the baseline. When the first short ball is hit, *all four* players must rush to the net. Neither team is allowed to let the ball bounce for the rest of the rally.

 The team who hit the short ball must attempt to volley an approach shot, probably from the mid-court – a real pressure situation.

TWO VOLLEYS WIN

Play doubles points. If the server's partner volleys two shots back into court (neither need be a winner) the serving team wins the point.

 The server's partner must be active to threaten and pressurize the receiver, while the receiver must try to keep the ball away from him.

NET REWARD

Play doubles points. If a team wins with a volley or smash, they score two points; they score one point for winning the rally with any other shot.

 In doubles it is important to keep up the net attack. Even if you lose points from the net in the early stages of a match, keep piling pressure on to the opponents by coming forward.

SHORT RALLY REWARD

Play doubles points. If a team wins the rally before five shots have been played (i.e. four shots or less in the rally), they score two points. They score one point if they win when five or more shots have been played.

 The best way to win a doubles rally quickly is for both players to get to the net position.

DOUBLES MISCELLANEOUS

The following exercises can challenge players of all standards. They focus on practising concepts that are important in doubles play, in most cases while actually playing doubles.

THREE IN A ROW

Play doubles where either team has to win three rallies in a row in order to score one point.

 This exercise encourages players to concentrate during every rally and to focus on consistent play.

SHORT WIDE COURT

Play points using the area between the service line and the net, including the doubles lines.

This exercise can be played on the basis that every ball must be allowed to bounce before it is returned, or alternatively that the ball is not allowed to bounce before it is returned.

 The emphasis is on touch, angles and keeping the ball low over the net.

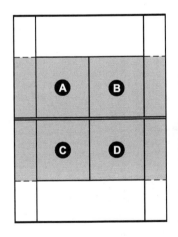

BACK DOWN

Play doubles points with normal scoring. If a team has a game point and they do not win it, they go back to 15. For example if the score is 40–15 to the serving team and the receiving team wins the next point, the score is 15–30.

 Finish the game at the first opportunity – deprive the opponents of second chances.

SENT OFF

Play doubles with five players per court, or four players and a coach. One player stands at the net post, waiting for the first rally to end. The player who is responsible for losing the point comes out and stands at the net post. The player who was waiting comes in and serves. Each player starts with ten points and loses a point each time he comes out.

 The player who misses the final shot of a rally is not necessarily 'responsible' for losing the point. For example, Player A hits a weak lob and the opponents smash it at A's partner…

This exercise often leads to useful discussions about which player has to leave the court and why.

SINGLES DOUBLES

Players A and B play 'singles doubles' or 'ghost doubles'. All shots must be hit crosscourt into the shaded area.

 Most shots in doubles are crosscourt.

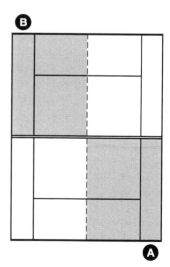

STAY IN

Play doubles where no player is allowed put a foot outside the lines, except the server for the start of the point.

 Players are encouraged to get to the net and to use angled shots – two central concepts in good doubles play.

ISOLATION

Play doubles, Team A versus Team B. The coach nominates one of the players on Team A as the 'stronger' player for the upcoming rally. If the nominated player hits more than two shots into court during the rally, Team A automatically wins the point.

 Keeping the ball away from the stronger player is standard practice in doubles.

THE TWO-VERSUS-ONE SESSION

Everyone benefits if a coach organises a competition day during the coaching term. The players enjoy it, while the coach can assess how the players' games are developing. Theory is translated into practice and the next progressions for the group can be plotted. In a two-on-one session, the two can practice doubles formations, while the single player benefits from the overload/pressure aspect of competing against two opponents.

DISMISSED!

Player A versus Players B and C. If A wins the point, he can 'dismiss' either B or C for the next point, and the player who is dismissed stands off the court. Let's say Player B has been dismissed. If his partner, Player C, wins the next point, B comes back on for the following point. If Player A beats Player C when C is alone, C goes off and B comes back on for the next point. Effectively what happens is that A plays against one opponent if he wins the previous point and against two if he loses the previous point.

 Will Player A choose to dismiss the stronger player each time? What is his tactical thinking?

DEFEND VERSUS TWO

Player A versus Players B and C. To win a point, A only has to return six shots in the rally. Players B and C must attack, while A defends and possibly counter-attacks.

 The emphasis is on Players B and C getting to the net – as in doubles.

TAKE TURNS

Player A versus Players B and C. The singles court is used, and Players B and C must hit alternate shots.

 A must be aware of his opponents' positions on court just before he hits each shot, so he can hit away from the player whose turn it is.

2:1

Player A versus Players B and C. To win the game, Player A must win five rallies, but B and C must win ten rallies.
• Player A could be asked to serve or to receive.
• Player A could be asked to hit into the singles court or the doubles court.

 The player by himself will be motivated to compete, since victory is a distinct possibility due to the scoring system.

RETURN V 2

Player A versus Players B and C. Player A only covers half the doubles court (whichever side he normally receives from in doubles). Players B and C do all the serving.

 This exercise provides intensive return-of-serve practice for the receiver.

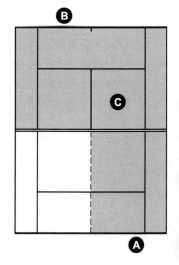

SERVE V 2

Player A versus Players B and C. Player A only covers half the doubles court. He serves alternately to Players B and C, and covers only the half of the court he served from. Player A serves all the time.

 This exercise provides intensive doubles serve practice for the server.

SMALL COURT CHALLENGE

Player A versus Players B and C. While B and C must cover the doubles court, Player A covers only half the width of the singles court.

 Players B and C are challenged to be accurate, while Player A will hit a lot of shots, since it will be difficult for his opponents to hit winners into such a small court.

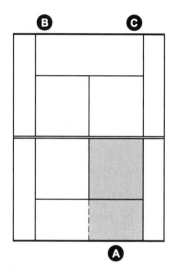

TO B OR NOT TO B

Player A versus Players B and C. If Players B and C win the rally before B has hit two shots, they do not score a point. Who has the most points after ten rallies?

 Player A needs to know where B is on the court and keep the ball away from him, while Player B is encouraged to be very active around the court.

PART SIX:
STRATEGY AND TACTICS

FORMULATING STRATEGY AND TACTICS

PLAYING STANDARD: ITN 10-5

In many sports, the manager or coach can speak to the players during breaks in play, or even communicate with them from the sidelines while play is in progress. With few exceptions, this is not the case in tennis. Players must be able to develop their own strategy and tactics in order to make the best use of their weapons, while frustrating the opponent's ambition to do likewise.

SWITCH

Players play points, holding the racquet in their non-racquet hand. They can use their 'good' hand for only one shot per rally.

 Does the player choose the correct time to switch the racquet to his stronger hand?

DO TELL...

Two players play points. Before each rally begins, each player must tell his partner, who is standing at the back fence, his plan for the upcoming rally. Players score one point if they win the rally and a bonus point if they have followed the plan as outlined.

 In the average match, the ball is in play only 20 per cent or 25 per cent of on-court time (less than 25 minutes in a ninety minute match). There is plenty of time between points and games to think and plan.

PERCENTAGE GAME

Two players rally. At any point in the rally, the coach can call 'Stop'. Players are asked to say what their chances were of winning the rally at the point it was stopped – 60:40 to win the rally, 90:10 etc. Discuss what each player should do next and why in order to finish the rally if he is in a strong position, or to get back into it if he is in trouble. Then play on the rally from where paused.

 Sometimes a player thinks he is in a good position to win the rally, but the coach does not agree! Discussing the situation provides a great learning opportunity for the player.

EXPLOIT THE WEAKNESS

Playing singles points, each player has a designated 'weakness' in his game. It does not need to be a real weakness, just something agreed for the purpose of the exercise – for example, backhand groundstroke for Player A and smash for Player B. If either player can make his opponent hit three of his designated weak shots in the rally, he wins the point immediately.

 Hitting to an opponent's weakness also implies keeping the ball away from his strengths, and is fundamental to winning tennis at all levels.

COUNSELLING SESSION

Play sets where each player has another member of the group who acts as coach and sits with the player at the changeover to discuss what to do in the next game.

 Many (especially young) players just hit the ball without a specific plan. You have to plan a meal, a journey, a study session – why should a tennis match be different?

This exercise benefits both the player and the 'coach'. Both are encouraged to look closely at what is happening on court and react to it.

OBSERVE, ANALYSE

Two players complete a set of singles. After the set, the coach discusses (one on one) what each player has discovered about his opponent's strengths and weaknesses.

 After a full set, each player should be able to provide quite a detailed analysis of his opponent's likes and dislikes, patterns of play, strongest shot etc.

OBSERVE, ANALYSE, ACT

Each player formulates a plan based on what he has discovered during the exercise above. Play another set to give the players an opportunity to implement their plan.

 It is an acknowledged fact that even the top players in the world have relative weaknesses in their game.

OBSERVE, ANALYSE, ACT, REVIEW

Having played the second set as described in the exercise above, the players assess the effectiveness of their plan with the coach (one on one) and decide whether to continue as it is or make adjustments.

 It is important that each player is aware of his opponent's strategy and tactics, and factors in how to prevent the opponent implementing his plan.

PLAYING STANDARD: ITN 10-6

From a player's first lesson, the strategic and tactical elements of tennis should be emphasised. Technique and tactics go hand in hand from the very beginning. The concept of hitting away from an opponent is quickly and easily understood by players of all ages.

THROW TO MOVE

Play singles in the four service boxes, throwing the ball rather than hitting. Each player throws the ball from wherever he is on the court when he catches his opponents 'shot'.

 Players quickly learn to vary placement and pace to move the opponent.

THE CIRCLE GAME

Player A feeds a ball to Player B, who must hit a shot that lands in the court and that A cannot catch. Player A must stay inside the circle. See how many points B can score from twenty feeds; then change roles.

 Increase the size of the circle as the players become more proficient.

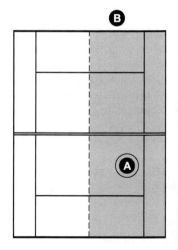

RUN AND CATCH 1

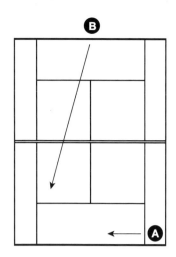

Player A stands just outside the singles sideline and feeds a ball to Player B. Once B contacts the ball, Player A runs into court and tries to catch it. If he does not catch it before the bounce or after one bounce, and the ball lands in the singles court, Player B scores a point. See how many points B can score from twenty feeds; then change roles.

 Rather than simply catch the ball, to prevent his opponent scoring a point Player A could be asked to either tip it with his racquet or return it into play.

RUN AND CATCH 2

This exercise has the same set up as 'Run and Catch 1' above, except that Player A feeds in the first ball from the centre of his baseline. This makes it more challenging for Player B to hit a shot that A cannot catch, touch or return.

 Some players need to be reminded that they can use the length as well as the width of the court to make their opponent run.

WIDE SERVE

Player A serves to Player B. If B does not return the ball, A wins the point. If Player B does return the serve, A does not score. However, B must stay inside the continuation of the doubles sideline, which for the purposes of this exercise is marked with throw-down lines. See how many points A can score from twenty serves; then change roles.

This is a useful exercise to underline the value of the slice serve when the right-hander is serving to the deuce court.

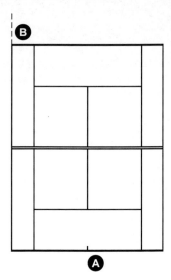

FOOT FAULT

Players A and B rally, with either player scoring one point anytime he can make his opponent put a foot past the singles sideline. Since players can score several points in one rally, the coach or a third player helps by keeping the score.

Players can be very effective at moving the opponent off the court by hitting shorter rather than deeper shots.

MOVING THE OPPONENT 2

The more steps an opponent must take to play a shot, the greater the chance that he will miss or play a weak return. Even if he does get it back, you have created space into which you can hit your next shot.

FAR, FAR AWAY

Player A feeds a ball to B, who hits a shot as far from A as he can. Count how many steps Player A must take to catch the ball.

 The players should attempt this exercise with Player B hitting from various positions on the court – which is most effective?

ONE RACQUET DOUBLES

Play doubles in the four service boxes. Each team has only one racquet and must play alternate shots. Players pass the racquet to their partner after they play a shot.

 A useful exercise for learning to exploit angles by hitting away from the player whose turn it is.

DOWN THE LANE 1

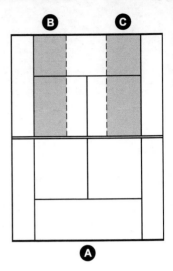

The court is divided into three lanes using drop-down lines. Player A rallies with Players B and C. The rally ends if A hits into the central lane. Player A can also be asked to hit alternately to B and C.

 Too many players hit too many shots down the middle.

DOWN THE LANE 2

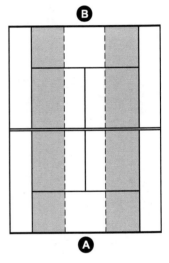

A central lane is marked out over the whole length of the court. Play points where the ball is out if it lands in the central lane.

 Move an opponent to tire him – this can make a big difference towards the end of a match.

DOUBLE POINTS

Playing singles and keeping the score numerically, either player scores two points if they hit a shot that their opponent cannot reach until it bounces twice or more. They score one point if the rally is won any other way.

 Hitting many clean winners can have a damaging effect on the opponent's morale.

TRAFFIC LIGHTS

The court is divided into three lanes, as in the diagram. Red, green and yellow cones are used to 'name' the lanes. If the players hit into the same lane twice in a row, they lose the point.

 An interesting addition to this exercise is to ask a player to call 'red', 'green' or 'yellow' before he hits the shot, depending on where he intends it to land. If it does not land in the lane designated, he loses the point.

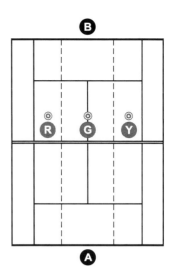

SAFE RISK

Either player scores two points if he hits a winner wide of the markers. If a ball is hit wide, the player does not lose the point – it is replayed.

The players are encouraged to take risks, but with the safety net of not losing the point for hitting wide.

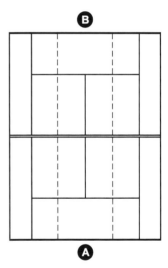

STOP THE ATTACK

This session reveals a lot about a player's understanding of both when to attack and how to prevent an opponent from attacking. It can be used for singles or doubles. During a match, a player must be able to analyse his opponent and what he is attempting to do. If the player is regularly attacked when he plays a particular shot or finds himself in a certain situation, he must recognise the problem and prevent it from recurring.

CAUGHT OUT 1

Players A and B play points. When A hits a shot that B feels he can attack, B catches the ball. Player A tries to prevent his opponent catching the ball by hitting shots that prevent B moving to attacking mode.

 Does Player A notice which shots Player B is attacking? These are the ones that need to be improved and changed.

Does Player A react correctly when he sees which shots his opponent tends to attack?

CAUGHT OUT 2

Repeat the exercise above, but on different court surfaces (slow, medium and fast). Players are asked to note how the characteristics of the playing surface change the attacking opportunities.

 What is the average length of rally on each of the different surfaces before Player B catches the ball?

CAUGHT OUT 3

Repeat the exercise above, but with Player A competing against different types of players – baseliners, net players, all-court players.

These exercises reveal a lot not only about Player A, but also about his opponent. Is he attacking (i.e. catching) off the right type of shots?

WITHOUT THE CATCH

Players A and B play points. If an opportunity to attack arises, they take it – play on rather than catch the ball. After a few games, the players should be able to say which of their shots the opponent is attacking most frequently. They then develop a plan to prevent the opponent attacking these shots. Play on to see if the plan is effective.

A player does not need a coach to tell him what his weak areas are – his opponent will let him know by attacking them.

LAST LINE OF DEFENCE

Certain situations develop during a rally where one player has a very good chance of winning the point with his next shot. This session puts players in some of these situations, whether as attacker or defender. During a match, winning a point from a seemingly impossible situation can have a positive psychological effect on the player who wins it and a negative one on the opponent.

WEAK LOB

Player A is at the net; B is at the baseline. The coach feeds a weak lob to A, who has an easy putaway smash. To score one point, Player A must win three rallies in a row. To score one point, B need only win one rally.

 Player B is encouraged to anticipate.

LOB VOLLEY

Players A and B are at the net, volley rallying. Player A hits a good lob volley – he should win the rally. He scores one if he wins the rally, but Player B scores three if he wins the rally. First to twelve points wins.

 The lob is the percentage shot for Player B when he goes to retrieve the ball over his head.

For safety, Player B is not allowed to smash the lob volley, even if he could do so.

FOREHAND PUTAWAY

Players A and B rally from the baseline. Player B delivers a short, high ball to A's forehand. Player A has an easy winner. He scores one point if he wins the rally, but B scores three points if he wins. First to twelve points wins the game.

 Can B influence where A places the ball by 'faking' – moving just before Player A makes contact with the ball?

HIGH VOLLEY PUTAWAY

Player A is at the net; B is at the baseline. Player B hits a poor passing shot (high to the forehand side) and then must try to recover and win the point from this weak position. He scores three points if he wins the rally and his opponent scores one point if he wins. Play to twelve points.

 Sometimes in these situations the player with the easy shot will try to make it too good – hitting very hard or very near the line. Only do as much with the ball as is necessary to win the rally.

ATTACKING A SHORT BALL

A short ball in tennis is like a penalty in soccer or a free throw in basketball – an excellent opportunity to score. When a player hits short, his opponent should quickly move forward and play an approach shot, a drop shot or a winner. Which shot to select will depend on:
- The height of the short ball;
- The position of the opponent;
- The player's favoured shot in this situation;
- The opponent's strengths and weaknesses;
- The opponent's expectations – counter-anticipate by choosing a shot other than the one he expects.

OPTIMISE YOUR POSITION

The coach at the baseline feeds a mixture of short and deep balls to the player on the opposite baseline. When the coach feeds short, the player must move forward quickly and catch the ball in his hand at the optimum height (higher rather than lower).

 Early perception that the ball is short, followed by quick movement forward, will allow the attacker to meet the ball at the best height and distance from the net.

APPROACH AND VOLLEY

Player A feeds a ball to Player B, who returns a short ball. Player A attacks the short ball with an approach shot. Play out the point.

 Most approach shots should be hit down the line.

GO FOR IT

Player A feeds a ball to Player B, who returns a short ball. Player A attacks the short ball by going for a winner.

 Winners are best attempted off higher bouncing balls.

When going for a winner, hitting crosscourt has greater potential to pull an opponent off the court.

DROP IT

Player A feeds a ball to Player B, who returns a short ball. Player A attacks the short ball by playing a drop shot.

 The drop shot may not be as effective in this exercise as in a match, since Player B knows it is coming.

YOUR CHOICE

Player A feeds a ball to Player B, who returns a short ball. Player A attacks the short ball with his choice of the three possibilities: approach, winner or drop shot.

Player A is now engaged in shot selection – does he make the right selection?

Very little time is available in which to make a choice, so the decision must be well trained.

IF AND WHEN

Players A and B rally, each trying to force the other to hit a short ball. If and when a short ball is hit, whoever receives it attacks, using one of the three possible shots. Play out the point.

 The exercise is realistic and close to matchplay because neither player knows when a short ball will be hit.

To get *short* balls, hit *deep* balls.

ATTACK THE SERVE

Players A and B alternate hitting second serves. The receiver attempts an approach shot, drop shot or winner as his return of serve.

 By definition every serve in play is a short ball. Players should practice all the above skills in the return of serve situation for use against weaker serves.

ATTRIBUTES OF A STRONG PLAYER

PLAYING STANDARD: ITN 7-4

The games of strong players have characteristics that constantly come to the surface during a match. These players also avoid other less desirable characteristics. This session provides players with an opportunity to discover which of these attributes of a strong player they possess and which they need to develop.

BASELINE WINNERS

Strong players can hit clean winners from the baseline. A player scores two points if he hits a clean winner and one point for winning the rally in any other way.

 Although a clean winner in a match is worth only one point, hitting them regularly gives a player a great mental boost, while having the opposite effect on an opponent.

SERVE WINNERS

Strong players often hit winning serves and aces. Score two points for winning the rally with the serve and one point for winning the rally in any other way.

 This exercise also challenges the receiver to make every effort to return the serve into play.

NET WINNERS

Strong players can win from the net. Score two points for winning the rally with a volley or smash and one point for winning in any other way.

 Players should be encouraged to experiment with all three main opportunities for going to the net – serve and volley, approach off a short ball or approach off a weak serve.

EIGHT OR MORE

Strong players can have long rallies. Play points where eight deep shots in a row must be hit at the start of the rally before either player can score a point (use drop-down lines to mark the border between deep and short). If the rally breaks down before eight deep shots have been played, no point is scored.

 An alternative scoring system is that the opponent scores two points instead of one if his opponent misses before eight shots have been hit, and one point if nine or more shots have been traded before the rally ends.

FIVE OR LESS

Strong players can have short rallies. Play points where a player scores two points if he wins the rally before six shots have been played. If six or more shots have been played, he scores one point.

 At the higher levels, players must create and then seize opportunities to attack as early as possible in a rally.

What type/placement of serve will produce the sort of opportunity necessary to allow a player to finish the point in three or four shots?

NO UEs

Strong players rarely make unforced errors. A player scores two points if his opponent makes an unforced error and one for a forced error.

 A player who makes few unforced errors puts his opponent under pressure to take risks in order to win the point.

This exercise often leads to useful discussions along the lines of, 'Was that a forced or unforced error?'

NO DOUBLE FAULTS

Strong players rarely double fault. The opponent scores two points if the server double faults and one if he wins the rally in any other way.

 A double fault is the worst type of unforced error, since the opponent has had to do nothing at all to win the point.

Recording the score – a note for coaches:
To tie this session neatly together, use a whiteboard hooked to the fence to keep each player's score in each of the seven 'attributes of a strong player'. Run each exercise for ten minutes and have the players change opponents after each exercise.

	Baseline Winners	Serve Winners	Net Winners	Eight or More	Eight or Less	No UEs	No Double Faults	TOTAL
Jack	12	14						
Helen	10	12						
Bill	8	6						
Jane	15	9						

PART SEVEN:
IN THE MIND

INTRODUCTION TO ANTICIPATION

Given the pace at which tennis is played today, anticipation skills are vital. Anticipation is defined as 'the ability to act before another, often so as to thwart [...] to foresee and deal with in advance'. It really boils down to an educated guess.

From early in their development, players should be exposed to situations where they need to anticipate. The exercises in this chapter are designed to provide practical on-court opportunities for kick-starting this process.

TOP OR SLICE

Players watch the coach and another player rallying. Before the coach hits the ball, the players call out 'topspin' or 'slice' – whichever spin they feel the coach is going to use.

 Encourage players to look at the grip, the backswing and the angle of the racquet face.

LISTEN

Players turn their backs to the coach, who hits a mixture of flat and spin shots at various speeds. After each shot, the players must say what type of shot it was – for example, 'flat and hard'.

 The sound of the racquet meeting the ball provides an early cue as to what type of shot is coming.

LEFT OR RIGHT

Players watch the coach hit groundstrokes. Before the coach hits the ball, the players call out 'Left' or 'Right' as to where on the court they think the ball will bounce.

 Alternatively the coach can ask the players to call 'Line' for a down-the-line shot or 'Cross' for a crosscourt shot.

WHERE TO?

The coach hits a number of groundstrokes at different heights, speeds and spins. A player at the net catches the ball before it bounces. The other players must say where on the court the ball would have bounced if it had not been stopped (also the position of the second bounce).

 Spin, trajectory and pace must be taken into account as the receiving player starts his early movement towards the ball.

BALL PICK UP

Player A stands on the doubles sideline facing across the court. Player B is near the singles sideline, facing Player A. There is a tennis ball on the singles sideline between the two players. Player B has to pick up the ball, then turn and run to the opposite singles sideline, without Player A being able to tip him. Player B is allowed to fake the pick up in order to throw his opponent off balance. Player A cannot move until Player B has picked up the ball.

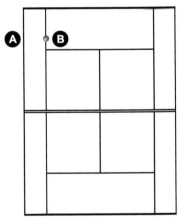

 Player A tries to get inside B's mind – looking at his eyes and body movements.

He should also watch out for patterns that may emerge when the two players have performed the exercise a number of times.

PASS OR LOB

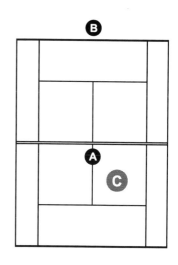

Player A stands at the net, Player B at the baseline. The coach stands behind player A and signals to Player B that he should hit a passing shot (finger pointing down) or a lob (finger pointing up). The coach then feeds the ball to Player B. The player at the net must call 'Pass' or 'Lob' before Player B makes contact with the ball.

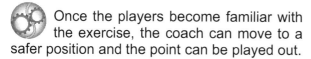 Once the players become familiar with the exercise, the coach can move to a safer position and the point can be played out.

Similar exercises can be developed using shots other than pass and lob. For example, a player at the net is required to play either a drop volley or a deep volley, or a player receiving a short ball is required to play either a winner or a drop shot.

SPOT THE PATTERN

The coach instructs one player to hit to a pattern (for example, all slice backhands must be hit crosscourt). How long before his opponent notices the pattern?

 Finding patterns (if any) is important in the anticipation process.

SCOUTING

Players A and B play points, while a third player scouts Player B, collecting as much information about his game as he can. The scout shares his findings with Player A, who plays on and tries to use the information gathered.

 Knowledge is power; forewarned is forearmed.

DEUCE OR VAN?

A player (the receiver) stands in the middle of the court at the baseline, near the centre mark. Another player (the server) is in the same position on the other end of the court. The server serves wide to either the deuce or advantage courts. The receiver must anticipate which box the server intends to serve to and move in that direction before the server contacts the ball. Otherwise he will have no chance to return the serve successfully.

 Does the server provide any technical cues – for example, the position of the toss?

ATTACK OR RALLY?

Player A feeds a wide ball to B, designed to make him run. Player A then immediately moves towards the centre of the baseline (ready to rally) or into the net position (ready to attack). Whether Player A moves to the baseline or net position depends on what he *anticipates* Player B will be able to do with his next shot and how strong it will be.

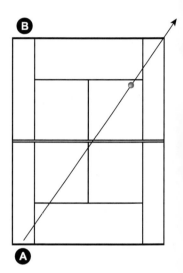

 A knowledge of what an opponent can and cannot do, based on his abilities and his position on court, makes the anticipation process faster and easier.

RAINY DAYS

Show a recording of a match from the pro tour. Press pause just before a player hits a shot. The coach asks the group where they think the next shot is going and why.

 This exercise is an ideal rainy-day activity.

ADVANCED ANTICIPATION

The lightening fast thought processes that enable a player to calculate in advance his opponent's next move, often with devastating effect, is one of the most interesting and exciting aspects of tennis. The following exercises provide players with multiple opportunities to work on anticipation (and counter-anticipation) skills. In each drill, the coach feeds a ball to Player A so that A has a relatively easy opportunity to win the point. As a result, Player B is forced to anticipate. This in turn encourages Player A to counter-anticipate.

Two possible scoring systems can be used for each of the following exercises:

- The player who has to anticipate (B) scores three points if he wins the rally. The player with the easy winner (A) scores one point if he wins the rally.
- Alternatively, Player B scores one point if he gets his racquet to the ball off Player A's first shot, even if he cannot get it back into play. He scores two points if he gets Player A's first shot back into play, even if he subsequently loses the rally. He scores three points if he wins the rally. Again, A scores one point if he wins the rally.

EASY FOREHAND

The coach feeds a high, short ball bouncing at X. Player A has a high mid-court forehand put-away. Player B must anticipate.

 Anticipation is often used in a no-hope situation. If you wait to see where your opponent's next shot is going, you will have no chance to get it. Anticipating gives you a 50 per cent chance.

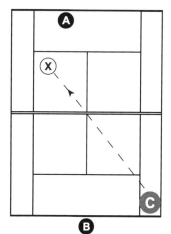

EASY PASS

The coach feeds a short ball bouncing at X. Player A has an easy passing shot. Player B must anticipate.

Even if a player anticipates wrongly, it puts pressure on an opponent by forcing him to second guess on future points.

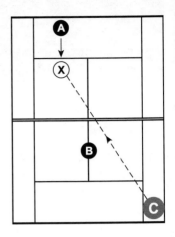

EASY SMASH

The coach feeds a short lob to Player A, who has an easy smash. Player B must anticipate.

Faced with a situation that requires anticipation, players should ask themselves the $64,000 question: 'What would I do next if I was my opponent?'

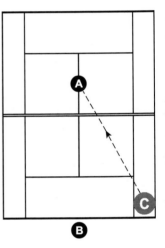

EASY VOLLEY

The coach feeds a shoulder-high volley to Player A, who aims at either target 1 or 2. Player B must anticipate.

Getting inside another player's mind is central to successful anticipation. It is also very disconcerting for the opponent.

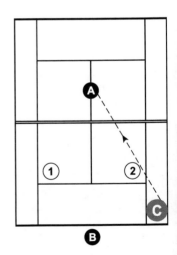

CONCENTRATION

Concentration is 'the ability to direct one's attention to a single object'. In a tennis match, one momentary lapse in concentration can have a significant effect on the outcome.

Most practice sessions take place in almost ideal situations – no spectators, no bad calls, no real pressure to win. When a player gets into a match situation, all this changes. His ability to ignore the many possible distractions will be improved if he can increase his experience of playing in an environment where there are diversions with the potential to break his concentration.

Concentration is effectively a process of selective attention: a player receives relevant and irrelevant information and the irrelevant must be filtered out.

RIGHT BECOMES LEFT

Right-handers play with their left hand and vice versa.

 Only excellent concentration will allow a rhythm to be achieved.
Less accomplished players can perform this exercise in the service box area.

IGNORING IS BLISS

Players A and B rally baseline to baseline. Other players face each other across the width of the court, standing outside the doubles lines, and rally parallel to the net.

The baseline players must block out the balls crossing their line of vision.

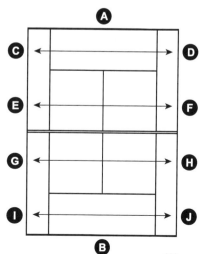

123

'CHALK FLEW UP'

Sets are played with a squad member or coach acting as umpire. The umpire deliberately makes bad calls, especially on key points.

 Players must learn to play the call, without becoming upset.

SOME PEOPLE...

Two players rally baseline to baseline. At the back of the court, on both ends, other squad members chat to each other loudly, tell jokes, bounce balls etc.

 Which pair can achieve the highest rally under these circumstances?

GAMESMANSHIP

The coach plays a tiebreak with the player, using all the tricks of gamesmanship. He stands on the wrong side to receive serve, re-ties his shoelaces after every second rally, talks to his opponent at every opportunity, is not ready to play when his opponent is ready and regularly argues about the score.

 There are players out there who behave like this, so all players need to learn to deal with it.

CROSSROADS

The coach schedules the lesson for the noisiest court in the club, where people are constantly passing by, crossing behind the court etc.

 Coaches often seek out the quietest court on which to teach, but is this helpful for their students?

PUPILS GIVE THE LESSON!

PLAYING STANDARD: ITN 7-4

A coach should occasionally allow the pupils to set up and run the day's session. It helps the players develop the independence they need to be successful. Because of the nature of tennis as an individual sport, players need to be able to organise and run their own practice sessions. These sessions also allow the coach to check his pupils' knowledge and understanding of the topic in question, thereby assessing the effectiveness of the coaching and creating an opportunity to discover what to do next.

A further benefit of this session is that it allows the players to see just how challenging the job of the coach really is!

SELECT AND PLAN

Working in pairs, players select a topic they will develop together, then deliver on court in the form of a short coaching session. They plan their session on paper – how and what to demonstrate, points to make during the demonstration, safe and effective exercises, and a brief summary for the finish.

 Working in pairs serves to take the pressure off the individual 'player coach'.

IMPLEMENT

Each pair takes their turn as coaches, giving a short lesson on their chosen subject.

 The coach must watch out for potentially dangerous situations, which can easily develop when someone is 'coaching' for the first time.

REVIEW

The 'player coaches'; the pupils and the coach get together to discuss the pros and cons of the session.

 In leading this discussion the coach should concentrate on the positive aspects of the session, since this is a vulnerable time for the player coaches.